A JOURNEY
OF
LITERARY AND ARCHAEOLOGICAL RESEARCH
IN
NEPAL AND NORTHERN INDIA,
DURING THE WINTER OF 1884-5.

A JOURNEY
OF
LITERARY AND ARCHAEOLOGICAL RESEARCH
IN
NEPAL AND NORTHERN INDIA,
DURING THE WINTER OF 1884-85.

BY

CECIL BENDALL, M.A.

FELLOW OF GONVILLE AND CAIUS COLLEGE, CAMBRIDGE; PROFESSOR OF SANSKRIT IN UNIVERSITY COLLEGE, LONDON; MEMBER OF THE ROYAL ASIATIC SOCIETY.

GYAN

Published by

Gyan Publishing House
5, Ansari Road
Daryaganj, New Delhi-110002
Phone: 011-47034999, 9811692060
E-mail: books@gyanbooks.com

Distribution Network
gyanbooks.com
India, USA, Canada, UK, Australia, France

ISBN : 978-81-212-3649-2 (PB)
First Published, 1886

2nd Impression 2020

Printed at: Gyan Press, Delhi.

A Journey of Literary and Archaeological Research
in
Nepal and Northern India,
During the Winter of 1884-5.
Author: Cecil Bendall

A JOURNEY

OF

LITERARY AND ARCHÆOLOGICAL RESEARCH

IN

NEPAL AND NORTHERN INDIA,

DURING THE WINTER OF 1884-5.

BY

CECIL BENDALL, M.A.

FELLOW OF GONVILLE AND CAIUS COLLEGE, CAMBRIDGE;
PROFESSOR OF SANSKRIT IN UNIVERSITY COLLEGE, LONDON;
MEMBER OF THE ROYAL ASIATIC SOCIETY.

CAMBRIDGE:
AT THE UNIVERSITY PRESS.
1886

I.

1. TEMPLES AND BATHING-GHATS AT THE SHRINE OF PAÇUPATI, NEPAL.

2. ISLAND-PALACE IN THE LAKE AT OODEYPORE.

Photographed by the Author.

Frontispiece.

PREFATORY LETTER.

DEAR MR VICE-CHANCELLOR,

The following pages are intended to fulfil the promise made in my letter, published by your predecessor in the *University Reporter* of 26 May 1885, of submitting to the University a detailed account of my recent tour in India, in accordance with the conditions of Grace 2 of the Senate of 19 June 1884. I then expressed a hope that the present publication might be ready early in last Michaelmas term; but circumstances rendered that impossible, and even now it is not as full as I could have wished. It seemed better however to make no further delay. The chief matters postponed are the descriptions of several interesting and little-known MSS. and the publication of several inscriptions.

In the descriptions of the new literature that I have brought to light, I fear my brief notices will seem very partial and meagre, if compared, for instance, with the admirable accounts and extracts given in the recent reports of Professors Peterson and Rāmakṛishṇa Bhāṇḍārkar. Some allowance will doubtless be made for the difference of situation between scholars working with the ever-helpful pandit always at hand in the glorious λαμπρὸς αἰθήρ of India, and the single-handed efforts of one whose hours of daylight (such as it is in a London winter) are chiefly consumed by official work. I have thus had to forego describing in detail the fine representative collection of Sanskrit and Prakrit literature purchased by me at Bombay from Pandit Bhagvān Dās, and to confine myself to reproducing his rough list without classifying the MSS., as I have done in the case of my own collection. Still less have I been able to give notes on the more remarkable works, as I have attempted in that case. An adequate description, indeed, would be the work of years rather than of months. My want of daylight leisure has also prevented me publishing all my inscriptions; but I hope to be able to deal with them before very long.

My acknowledgments of help received during the journey itself will be found at the end of Part I. In reading these, I trust my native friends will recognise their own names. At the risk of occasionally seeming pedantic, I have transliterated their names like other Indian words, without reference to local pronunciation[1].

In the preparation of the present work, I have to thank several friends, especially Professor William Wright, for many valuable hints and for kind and prompt help in revising the proofs. Professor J. G. Bühler of Vienna has likewise aided in the revision of my inscriptions. Professor Cowell, Dr Daniel Wright, Professors Weber, Jacobi, and Adams have also favoured me with ready answers to various special questions that I have ventured to address to them.

I feel it also my sad duty to refer here to not fewer than three of those who aided in my work in various ways, and have been removed by death since I commenced it.

The first is the late Raṇa-uddīpa Siṃha (Runoodeep Sing), Mahārāja (Prime Minister) of Nepal, who was slain during the disturbances in Kathmandu in November last. Whoever may be the new rulers, I trust they will be no less ready than the late Premier to afford a courteous reception to scholars.

Next I must mention Mr James Fergusson, incomparably the soundest and most accomplished critic of our day in his particular branch of art, who took a kindly interest in the journey now recorded, both before and after it was undertaken.

[1] As for Bengali, where the divergence of spelling and pronunciation is greatest, attempts to put them into 'popular' spelling appear often as ridiculous in the eyes of the Hindus as in our own, if we may judge from the correspondence in the "Pandit" for April 1869 (Vol. III. p. 248).

Perhaps one of the last opinions he delivered on his favourite subject of Indian art was in reference to the photograph of the temple at Oodeypore now published[1].

Lastly I have to mourn the heavy loss, still fresh in the mind of every Cambridge reader, of one of the most trusty, most energetic, and most appreciative friends and supporters of the present work, and, let me add, of the worker also. Under the auspices of Henry Bradshaw, the greatest librarian of our time, it was my privilege to commence my study of manuscripts. I shall never forget the sympathy, and even enthusiasm with which he used to follow, in the minutest palæographical and chronological details, my endeavours to arrange the great Nepal collection of our Library, nor my debt to him for many a hint and practical direction in the work of re-arranging many masses of confused leaves and in describing and registering the re-arrangement. I well remember a phrase of his, used not without a touch of irony significant for us librarians: "My favourite occupation is putting rubbish in order." Though no professed Orientalist, he had something to teach specialists in all branches. He had, as many others can testify, a very strong sense of the value of our Oriental collections, and not the least of that sent by Dr Wright from Nepal. My proposal to visit that country found in him from the first one of its most friendly and warmest supporters. I have seldom received more real encouragement than from the expression of the genial and firm support that he was pleased to give to my application to the Worts Fund on the occasion of its discussion in the Arts School on 17 June 1884.

Conscious as I am of the shortcomings of the present work, I have no keener regret in connexion with it than that it cannot be submitted to him at all events in its complete form, though some of the first part was read in manuscript by him and has been in a few places modified according to his suggestions. Yet it is some satisfaction to know his opinion of my efforts, and of their possible results and development, whether by

[1] See List of Illustrations, No. VII., note 2.

myself or others: and thus I feel that I cannot now do better than conclude by quoting the final sentences of the last letter of any consequence that he wrote to me,—à propos of the journey now described: "Your work is a real beginning and must lead to more good work. I only hope that you may be allowed to have a hand in it."

I remain,

dear Mr Vice-Chancellor,

Yours faithfully,

CECIL BENDALL.

To the Reverend the Vice-Chancellor of the University of Cambridge.

London, *March* 1886

TABLE OF CONTENTS.

LIST OF ILLUSTRATIONS.

COLLOTYPES (Autotype Company's process).

(*Except where otherwise stated, from negatives by the author.*)

[1] Not described in the text: but see Dr D. Wright's History of Nepal, p. 21.

[2] The two views from Oodeypore (I. 2 and VII) are also not described in the text, but are in fact inserted by an after-thought, the first as an attempt to give some idea of the wonderfully beautiful combination of architecture and lake-scenery, so characteristic of Rajputana, in a locality still surprisingly little known. As for the temple (No. VII), almost the only notice I find of it is in Major H. H. Cole's First Report on Ancient Monuments, p. clxxix, where he draws attention to its astonishingly late date, A.D. 1734. As the photographs illustrating this Report are not generally accessible, I publish this, though it is by no means all I could wish it to be, until a better appears. The condition of photography in India, I may here observe, is most unsatisfactory. The ordinary European firms charge for views prices that I may characterize, from knowledge of the actual cost of photography in the country, as most exorbitant. I found however one distinctly able and enterprising photographer, somewhat more moderate in charge, Lāla Dīn-dayāl, a Digambara Jain at Indore, who seems to have brought to bear on our modern art-science some of the traditional art-feeling of his sect. For the sake of those readers who are interested in Indian architecture I may mention that this photographer has a London agent, Mr Farrer of Hanway Street, W.

LITHOGRAPHS.

PART I.

ARCHÆOLOGICAL AND GENERAL REPORT.

My tour in Northern India commenced at Bombay on Oct. 22nd, 1884.

After landing I lost little time in making the acquaintance of Pandit Dr[1] Bhagvānlāl Indrajī, whose researches in Indian antiquities, chiefly published in the *Indian Antiquary*, are well known both in India and Europe. The Pandit resides near the Valkesvar shrine—a celebrated and most picturesque place of Hindu pilgrimage, situated in strange juxtaposition to the fashionable European quarter of the Malabar Hill. In his house is a large and interesting collection of coins, copperplate grants and other antiquities. Amongst other objects I may note in particular a double-headed figure covered with inscriptions in the rare and interesting Ariano-Pali character. It is much to be desired that the Pandit or some other antiquary should publish some account of this monument.

Having made no extensive study of Indian numismatics, I offer no opinion as to the exact value of the Pandit's collection of coins, which is however strongly representative of the Gupta period; but as the Pandit has probably made more extended scientific travels than any other native of India, and these

[1] The Pandit was presented with the honorary degree of Ph.D. by the University of Leiden, already distinguished for its Orientalism. I trust that our own Universities will some day do honour to themselves by following this example, especially if, as seems likely, some distinguished native scholars are induced to come to Europe for the Orientalists' Congress of next year.

always with an antiquarian object, it doubtless represents a great diversity of place as well as time. I have little doubt that Dr Bhagvānlāl would readily respond to requests from institutions like the University or the British Museum for copies or impressions, from which possibly exchanges of duplicates could be arranged.

My more particular purpose in seeking the acquaintance of this great scholar was to gain some advice as to my journey to Nepal. The Pandit himself spent four months in that country in the year 1880, and published some valuable and interesting inscriptions, copied by him there, in the *Indian Antiquary* (Vol. IX. pp. 160 seq., sequel in Vol. XIV. pp. 411 seq.). Following a suggestion of my friend Professor J. G. Bühler of Vienna, who had kindly written to Dr Bhagvānlāl to interest him in my journey to Nepal, I sought to induce him to accompany me thither; but after some hesitation my proposal was declined on the ground of numerous literary engagements. I may state here, however, that on my return to Bombay the Pandit expressed regret that he had not gone with me, and further added that, should I visit Nepal again, he would accompany me both to Kathmandu and to some other parts of the country, which I shall mention later on.

I cannot however speak in too warm terms of the kind and friendly way in which this eminent scholar placed at my disposal the very exceptional experience he had gained, as the only scientific traveller who had visited this secluded country unencumbered by all the restrictions placed there on Europeans. I not only profited by numerous conversations with him during my hurried stay in Bombay, but also received after my departure several letters containing valuable hints and information as to the whereabouts of objects whose existence the Pandit had ascertained without being able to publish a description of them.

In Dr Bhagvānlāl's collection are also several early MSS. from Nepal, from which I obtained some fresh dates supplementing the chronological table of the kings of Nepal occurring at pp. xii. sqq. of my Catalogue. These are given in Appendix III. below.

On leaving Bombay for the interior I made a short detour to the great cave of Kārli, certainly among the most solemn and impressive of all the temples of the world, deeply interesting as a monument alike of the stately magnificence of ancient Buddhism, and of constructive religious art, enhanced by the venerable records with which its stones are covered. After a preliminary visit to Benares I proceeded by the Tirhut State Railway to Motihāri. I passed the Nepalese frontier near Phulwaria, not without considerable annoyance from the officials, and arrived in Kathmandu[1] on November 9th.

Here I occupied the travellers' bungalow belonging to the Government of India, and during each day was entertained by the Resident, Mr C. Girdlestone, whose kind cooperation in forwarding several of the objects of my visit I desire cordially to acknowledge. The first of the few days I was enabled to spend in Nepal had to be given up to inactivity, as the Resident considered it unadvisable to visit the city, especially for the purposes of archæological search, without acquainting the Durbar with the objects of my mission. I utilized the time, however, to some extent in preliminary work for my chief object, the acquisition of MSS., by several conversations with the Residency Pandit Indrānand, the son of the late Pandit Guṇānand, one of the *collaborateurs* in the *History of Nepal* compiled by Dr Daniel Wright, and published by the University. Such success as I had in my main object was almost entirely due to the exertions of this Pandit, to whom I am also much indebted for very attentive and courteous guidance in visiting several of the more distant localities of archæological interest. I also

[1] I leave the spelling of this name without diacritical marks, because I do not care for such marks in geographical names where they are not absolutely necessary as guides to an intelligible pronunciation, also because there seems great doubt as to the exact form in this case. The native chroniclers seem always to use the quasi-classical form, Kāntipur; Dr Hunter's Gazetteer has 'Khatmandu (*Káthmándú*)'; another Sanskritised form (giving a real or attempted derivation) is Kāshṭhamaṇḍapa (see my Catalogue, p. 100); the writer of the recent history of Nepal in Bengali, a native of Nepal whom I met in his exile, writes Kāṭmuṇḍa. In any case, let me observe that the first syllable is long (a as in 'bath'), while the accent is on the second syllable.

profited much by the cordially rendered assistance of the Residency Mīr Munshi, Durgācaraṇa Miçra. The Pandit had already gained particulars as to a list of desiderata which I had forwarded to the Resident by post: he had also obtained one MS. on approval, which I ultimately purchased. See Classified List of MSS. in Part II., § XI. No. 2.

On the 12th November I made a beginning of practical archæological work by visiting some of the places in or near the town of Kathmandu in which inscriptions had been found by Pandit Bhagvānlāl in 1880.

The very first and nearest of these seemed to illustrate forcibly how desirable it is that opportunities should be taken to reproduce these documents while they still exist.

This was the short inscription of Aṃçuvarman [*Indian Antiq.* Vol. IX. (for August, 1880), No. 8], which is described as at Satdhārā near the Rāṇīpokhra tank. The whole masonry of the place round the spring seems quite recently to have been demolished, and heaps of brick rubbish are lying about in all directions, the whole spot as far as the tank being now included in the parade-ground. I found no trace of the inscription, so that it would seem that the Pandit was only just in time to preserve a record of it.

I next visited Lagan-ṭol, within the town, and there saw the originals of Nos. 3 and 4 of Pandit Bhagvānlāl's series, and can testify to the great accuracy of the published reproductions of these, as I examined the dates in particular with considerable care. Near the site of No. 4, at the opposite side of the temple of Jaisi, is a specimen of a class of inscription of which I found several instances in Nepal, viz., a stone at the end of a conduit in which was formerly a spout, inscribed with the date and name of donor. The present inscription is given in full in Appendix I. with facsimile. It is dated [Çrīharsha-] Saṃvat 151 (A.D. 657), and records the donation of the conduit with *certain measures* of land by a matron named Bhojamati to the temple-committee of Lanjagval for their perpetual enjoyment thereof.

On November 14th I visited the famous hill of Svayambhūnāth, of which a description, together with early myths

T. Way, Lith, London. From a Photograph by the Author

CAITYA OF SVAYAMBHUNĀTH.

NEPAL.

To face p. 5.

concerning it, is to be found in Dr D. Wright's work on Nepal, pp. 23, 79 sqq. I give a view, drawn from an imperfect negative of my own, of part of the great central mound, with a curious collection of smaller stūpas of slate and stone with which the courtyard is crowded. I ascertained from some of the priests of the shrine that several Sanskrit manuscripts, including a palmleaf 'Ashṭasāhasrikā,' a paper Lalitavistara and others, were preserved here. They declined, however, to exhibit them, the custom being to produce them only on special religious occasions for the adoration of the faithful. How intelligent would be the use of such books may be inferred from the circumstance that even the chief priest to whom I addressed some simple Sanskrit phrases, did not so much as attempt to answer me in the classical language—a point of honour with every decent pandit in the plains of India.

During my pilgrimage to the shrine I found remains of an early inscription on a fallen and broken lāṭ or votive pillar, now lying along the side of a well in the courtyard. It may be seen in the illustration just at the feet of the group of garlanded worshippers and others. The inscription is at present a mere fragment, as the lower part is broken, and the upper part is worn and has been partly recovered with a thinly scratched (and to me illegible) modern inscription. The character, however, of what remains is of decided Gupta type, quite distinct from the Aṃçuvarman group of the VIIth cent. A.D., as may be seen at once from the archaic forms of क, ष and other letters, which resemble typical inscriptions of the fourth and fifth centuries; so that we may fairly infer that the shrine has an antiquity of some 1400 or 1500 years—a consideration which is interesting when taken in connexion with the literature of the spot, namely the various redactions of the Svayambhū-Purāṇa, as to which it may suffice here to refer to the citations in my Catalogue of the Buddhist Sanskrit MSS. in the University Library, p. 7. Up to the present time I have not succeeded in obtaining from the few lines that are even partly legible anything of sufficiently connected interest to make it worth publishing. I also took a photograph (not now published) at the base of the great flight of steps leading up the hill, shewing a figure of Buddha between two lions of archaic character. The figures and numerous small stūpas here are surrounded by numbers of small tablets deposited by Tibetan pilgrims. Most of them bear the familiar 'om maṇi padme hūm' in the characteristic raised (not incised) letters. A living representative of these pilgrims was standing in the foreground.

In the latter part of the same day I was favoured with an interview with His Excellency the Mahārāja or prime minister of Nepal, Raṇa-uddīpa Siṃha. On the same occasion I had the pleasure of meeting General Khaḍga Shaṃsher Siṃha, who by his friendly courtesy and excellent knowledge of English was of great assistance to me on this and several other occasions. There was also present the Durbar pandit, Vācaspati, who conversed in clear and excellent Sanskrit, in which also the Mahārāja (who is evidently much interested in the classical language) occasionally joined.

I then explained my objects in visiting Nepal, briefly referring to the work recently done by myself and by others on the literature and antiquities of the country. Permission was granted to see the Durbar library and also to copy inscriptions and to photograph buildings. I also made some suggestions as to the desirability of viewing some very ancient manuscripts and other documents mentioned to me by Dr Bhagvānlāl Indrajī as in the possession of Buddhist and other religious establishments, and a promise was made that efforts should be directed towards procuring access to these, by having them brought to the Durbar or otherwise. Judging by the great trouble that was taken to show me the Mahārāja's own MSS., it may fairly be supposed that, had my stay in the country not been curtailed as it was, some of the hopes thus raised might have been realised. On the following day I visited Bodhnāth (described in Wright's *History* p. 22, with a picture[1], and the legend of its

[1] The place is really flat; the apparent elevation behind the mound is obviously due to a desire on the part of the Doctor's native draughtsman to get in as many buildings as he could.

foundation at p. 100). The shrine seems almost entirely kept up by Bhotiyas and Tibetans. The adjacent village abounds in small Tibetan inscriptions, mostly of very modern appearance. I took a rough copy of a single specimen of these.

On the 16th November I made my first visit to the interesting old town of Pātan, formerly called Lalitapur or Lalitapattan, only 2½ miles from Kathmandu, but long the seat of a separate monarchy[1], and at present the chief seat of the national Buddhism. A photograph is published by Hoffman of Calcutta, which gives some idea of the singularly diversified and picturesque effect of the group of temples in the great square of the old Durbar there. They appear to be mostly of the XVIth and XVIIth centuries: and from inscriptions written in Newari, and therefore not reproduced here, I gained some particulars as to the genealogies and dates of the kings of this period, which I have incorporated in the revised table of kings supplementary to that published in the introduction to my Catalogue. See Appendix III. In a street leading through a small drill-ground, eastwards from the south-east corner of this square, I discovered two inscriptions of the VIIth century, adjacent to wells called respectively Gairī-dhārā and Sun-dhārā.

The first is dated [Çrīharsha-] Saṃvat 82 (A.D. 688) and records the provision made by a monarch for the due worship of a divinity as well as for the repair and cleansing of the shrine. The residue (*pariçesha*), if any, of the grant was to be used for the feeding of 'the Pāçupatas and Brahmans.' The executive officer of the grant is a *Yuvarāj* whose name seems to be Skandadeva. The stone is much weather-worn at the top, but many of the remains of incisions, though nearly flattened down, are fairly legible. The experience of a stone like this showed the importance of supplementing any system of estampage or other copy from contact, by photography. At the same time I have unfortunately to add that the risks of the latter process were exemplified by the fracture of the glass of my negative, which I therefore do not publish, but give in Appendix I. an autotype

[1] See my *Catalogue of Buddhist Sanskrit MSS.*, Introd. p. x.

reproduction of part of the *back* of my paper copy, so that the letters appear raised instead of incised as they are in fact.

The Sundhārā inscription is dated [Çrīharsha-] Saṃvat 34 (A.D. 640) and records a grant, from a king whose name is now lost, but doubtless Aṃçuvarman, of land near the village of Māṭiṅ, the assessment (*piṇḍaka*[1]) of which is to be handed over to the Pāñcālikas, elsewhere endowed both by Aṃçuvarman and his successor Jishṇugupta (Bhagvānlāl, Inscr. 7 and 10), as a permanent endowment for the repair of a building which the king had recently restored after considerable dilapidations had occurred. As to who the Pāñcālikas were, we have no certain information. Dr Bhagvānlāl in his note (26) on his 7th inscription tells us that "the word *Pāñcālika* seems to be a technical expression corresponding to the southern Pāñcakulika and the modern 'Panch'": with which we are to compare the modern temple-committees called *guṭṭhī*. In the *History of Nepal* as translated by Dr D. Wright, the term does not seem to occur, but at p. 163 we find that (many centuries after this) a town Panāvatī (now Panautī) was founded 'near the Prayāga-tīrtha of Nepal, celebrated in the Shastras, on the site where the Pancāla-des formerly stood'; while on p. 133 we are told that Aṃçuvarman, who was reigning at the date of this inscription, "went to Prayāga-tīrtha and persuaded [the deity] Prayāga Bhairava to accompany him to Nepal." May we conjecture (until further evidence is forthcoming) from these confused and mythical traditions that the Pāñcālikas were a band of settlers, whom Aṃçuvarman introduced from the Kanauj and Prayāg (Allahabad) districts and whom he sought to propitiate by grants of territory and general endowment?

Near the inscription, on the opposite side of the open square in which it stands, is a small group of images in high relief with a votive inscription in verse recording that in [Nepal] Saṃvat 203, Vāṇadeva, son of a king (*bhūnātha*) Yaçodeva, erected this image in honour of the Sun-god, which had been

[1] See Bhagvānlāl's Inscriptions, foot-note 31.

II.

FIGURE OF SUN-GOD WITH INSCRIPTIONS (NO. V.)

planned by his mother. Two points of interest attach to this group, of which I accordingly made a photograph, now reproduced. (1) In view of the comparative rarity of sun-worship at the present day, it is important to get a dated figure of the deity with his attendants. In illustration of this I may mention that none of the pandits to whom I showed the photograph recognised the figure without the inscription, excepting only Dr Bhagvānlāl, who tells me that he means to publish some notes, which will surely be most acceptable, on sun-cult in India. (2) Yaçodeva being unknown as a king of Nepal proper, it is reasonable to suppose that he was a neighbouring petty rāja; as such he may have been the father of the first of the new line who about this time (Wright p. 160, and Bhagvānlāl, *Ind. Ant.* Dec. 1884) took possession of the Nepalese throne. It is true that the first of this line is called Vāma-(Bāma-)deva, not Vāṇadeva; but such errors of a letter where the sound is similar are not uncommon in these *vaṃçāvalīs*: thus Ānanda, known to us from the MS. colophons, is always called Nanda in the chronicles; so too his successor is variously called Mitra and Amṛita. I suppose, then, Vāṇadeva to have been at this time (A.D. 1083) intriguing (cf. Wright, l.c.) as *yuvarāj* with the people of Patan and to have enjoyed his two years of sovereignty about three or four years later. See Appendix III.

About 20 yards up a lane leading southwards from the same square is a conduit stone with a line or two of chipped and obliterated letters of archaic type.

The next day was occupied by second visits to the inscriptions near the Jaisi temple in Kathmandu and to Svayambhūnāth hill to further the investigations summarized above.

Nov. 18, 19. After a day spent chiefly in work connected with MSS., I walked to the charmingly situated shrine of Gokarṇa, and attempted to reach from thence the hill of Chāngunārāyaṇa, but being misdirected, had to postpone the visit to another opportunity, which, I regret to state, did not occur. I have written to Nepal, however, for a copy of the missing parts of Pandit Bhagvānlāl's reproduction of the important inscription there, and venture to hope that after the general progress made in the country since the Pandit's attempt seven years ago[1], no difficulties will now be experienced in getting the whole copied.

On Nov. 20 I visited Kīrtipur, but failed to find any early inscriptions; but on my return thence through the southern part of Kathmandu I discovered a conduit inscription in a place called Varam-ṭol. It is dated [Nepal] Saṃvat 259 (A.D. 1139), by a curious coincidence the same reign and date as Add. MS. 1643, second colophon, in our University Library. The characters have a special interest as being, I think, hitherto unnoticed in inscriptions and bearing a very distinct analogy to the hooked-top written character of the period, peculiar to Nepal, as to which I may be permitted to refer to my remarks in the Palæographical Introduction to my Catalogue of MSS. from Nepal. See Appendix I.

The language of the inscription is somewhat faulty in its Sanskrit and relates to the construction of the conduit.

Nov. 21. The archæological work of the next day was chiefly in Kathmandu.

Here I took a photographic view now produced in autotype of a portion of the great Durbar-square, often photographed from different points. I selected the Kumārī-deval at its S.W. corner as a typical Nepalese temple, showing in the background a building somewhat characteristic in style, which Dr D. Wright explains to me to be an annexe to the Durbar, used on ceremonial occasions.

Further I selected a stūpa in a court behind the houses in a narrow but busy street leading northwards from the square and called Eṭṭa-ṭol, as an example of this kind of erection still found even in the middle of the larger towns, and usually standing, as this one does, in large open squares which must be of great sanitary advantage in a place where to western notions every law of health seems reversed[2].

[1] See the *Indian Antiquary*, Vol. IX. 160.

[2] Dr Daniel Wright's remarks (*History of Nepal*, p. 12) are not at all too severe from a European doctor's point of view. I can only say that the con-

III.

KUMĀRĪ-DEVAL, KATHMANDU.

T. Way Lith, London.

From a Photograph by the Author.

KVACCHA-DEVAL, NEAR PATAN.

NEPAL.

In the vicinity I found an inscription dated [Nepal] Saṃvat 818 (A.D. 1698), reign of [Bhā]skaramalla (see Revised Table, Appendix III.).

Nov. 22. On this day a second visit to Patan yielded some of the results anticipated in the account of the place given above, and I also took occasion to photograph the Kvaccha-deval which stands outside the town to the N.E. and near the river. From my photograph a lithographic drawing has been made, which is now published. My visit to this temple was due to a drawing (No. 21) in a series prepared some 50 years ago for Mr Brian Hodgson, at once the greatest and least thanked of all our Indian Residents, when in charge at Kathmandu.

Mr Hodgson kindly lent me the series for my journey and the present report: and has directed that it is to be hereafter deposited in the India Office Library. I observe that in the drawing in question a smaller, two-storied, temple is added to the right hand of the large one. This is stated in a foot-note to be "Sacred to Sarasvati, built by Tejnám 567, Newar era"; but there is no trace of this building now. It would be interesting to learn how it disappeared; it was certainly not pulled down to gain room, as the temple stands quite beyond the town. It occurs to me as possible that Mr Hodgson's native draughtsman, a weak point with whom was trying to get too much into a picture, inserted a temple from some other place to make a pleasing composition. If I could make a longer visit to Nepal, I should certainly try to clear up this point, as 567 (A.D. 1447) is somewhat early for such a building as that shown in the drawing.

Near the N.W. corner of the town stands the temple of

dition of an ordinary eastern town, say Cairo or Benares, gives one no idea at all of Kathmandu. The nearest thing I found in India were some terrible lanes in the native capital (in most respects so 'advanced') of Jeypore. But as the people seem stronger and far more active than most of the inhabitants of India, sanitary criticism is a little disarmed. It would be certainly a pity, and moreover useless, as Dr Wright points out, to destroy the old buildings, often so charmingly picturesque, simply to apply laws made for a less hardy race. I am bound however to add, that since I left Kathmandu, and indeed since I wrote the above lines, a very severe outbreak of cholera has occurred in the town.

Kumbheçvara (Çiva), which I have selected for illustration as a fine and hitherto unnoticed specimen of Nepalese architecture. In the extensive and picturesque courtyard of this temple are several inscriptions. The earliest is clearly and evenly cut on a slab of slate, so smooth as to allow of my making a heel-ball copy. The inscription is dated in Nep. Saṃv. 512 (A.D. 1392), and records the foundation of the temple by one Jayabhīma to promote the recovery of his wife from a fever; Çiva however took her to his heaven; but the husband kept his word, and with the consent of his second wife Abhayalakshmī and his sons, built a lofty temple (prāsāda) to Çiva Kumbheçvara with *torans* (trabeate arches), in place of the mere dwelling-house (āvāsa) which had housed the god before. He likewise cleared the ground and surrounded it by walls, subsequently adding a square-built treasury (?) (chāturmukhakoça), which, as well as the temple, he enriched with precious ornaments. I had not time to work out fully the archaeology of this fine temple, but I noted on the main building a long inscription dated 921 (A.D. 1801), apparently referring to a restoration. See the autotype reproduction of my negative.

On the outskirts of the town are the Ipi-tūda chaitya-mound and the Ipi-vihāra. The former is of simple form and preserves the wooden poles which appear in Mr Hodgson's sketch of the place[1]. To the latter, which seemed a typical and ancient vihāra, I was not allowed entrance beyond the door. In all matters of this kind I always found the adherents of Buddhism—once the most liberal of religions—more superstitious than the lowest of the Hindus and as intractable as the most bigoted of the Jains of India.

Close to the above-named temple is a building, obviously a Buddhist vihāra, to which, as it has passed into the hands of Hindus, being now a "Bhagvan-deval," I gained access, and photographed the quaint courtyard, in which may be still seen all round the latticed apartments where the reading of the law

[1] Dr Wright does not give this chaitya any special name. It is No. 3 in his note on p. 116 of his history.

IV.

TEMPLE OF KUMBHEÇVARA, PATAN.

Photographed by the Author.

V.

DISUSED BUDDHIST MONASTERY, PATAN.

Photographed by the Author.

and other religious exercises were carried on. See the autotype reproduction.

On Nov. 23—24 I made a two days' visit to Bhātgāon, staying there in a house kindly placed at my disposal by H. E. the Mahārāja.

To the right of the temple of Bhairava, in one corner of the great square, I found an inscription of Yakshamalla dated N.S. 560 (A.D. 1440), of which I took a rough squeeze.

Near the celebrated brass gate of the palace I noticed an inscription of Raṇajitamalla, dated N.S. 874 (A.D. 1754), the latest date of any document that I have observed previous to the Gorkha conquest.

In this town I obtained direct access to a collection of MSS., several of which were in Bengali or in Maithili character and dated in the peculiar local Lakshmaṇa Sena Saṃvat (A.D. 1106). Amongst others I noted a copy of a rare grammatical commentary, the Bhāshāvṛitti by Purushottama, and portions of a work called Nyāyaçāstrasmṛiti written at Kathmandu in the VIth century of Nepal: a Newari commentary was added to the text and the work seemed similar to the 'Mānava-nyāya-çāstra' of Nārada, subsequently purchased by me at Kathmandu. In Dhruva-ṭol I found a small and fragmentary inscribed slab in the centre of a raised platform now chiefly used for threshing.

Further up the winding lane which forms the chief street of the town, in a place called Golmāḍhi-ṭol, I found another inscription in more perfect condition. This I have already published in the *Indian Antiquary* for 1885. As there stated, the inscription is to be compared with others of the same two rulers in the series already referred to (see the *Indian Antiquary*, Vol. IX. pp. 169 foll.) edited by Drs Bhagvānlāl and Bühler, which give the dates of Samvat 34 and 39, referred to the era of Çrīharsha and thus corresponding to A.D. 640—46. Independently of Nepalese evidence, we know from Hiuen Thsang that Aṃçuvarman flourished in the first half of the VIIth century A.D.; so that the date of the present inscription, 318, accords perfectly with Al-Berūnī's Gupta-Vallabhi era of A.D. 319[1], as we thus get for the inscription the date of A.D. 637, which admirably accords with what we know already of the two rulers just named. Compare now the continuation of the above-cited paper in the *Indian Antiquary*, Vol. XIII. p. 422, etc. I of course photographed this stone, and the reproduction from my negative is given with my transcript in Appendix I.

The other inscription, as far as it remains, is a duplicate of the same proclamation addressed to the same villagers, together with the inhabitants of several other districts, the boundaries of which are accurately given both by the cardinal points and by land measurements. A reproduction of a portion only of my squeeze of this inscription is given in Appendix I., and this merely on account of the dissimilarity of the *style* of character from the other. Though of course contemporaneous, the writing is freer and more sloping, and, so to say, cursive in effect.

Later on I took note of two more inscriptions: the first near the temple of Nārāyaṇa in Khaumār-ṭol, the second in a *math* or quasi-collegiate establishment, behind No. 12 Valacche-ṭol. I regret that the crowd of idle followers who pursued me into the quiet little courtyard where this inscription, with some others of later date, was fixed, so disturbed the tenants of the *math* that, on returning to take a copy, I found the door closed against me. I generally found, I may observe, that, in Nepal, where Tibetans and Chinamen attract no notice, the mere dress of a European is sufficient to draw a train of 30 or 40 idlers, which would soon be doubled if an object like a photographic camera were produced.

It may be noted in illustration of the force of Hindu customs in Nepal just as in the plains, that I observed during my walk through the town a picturesque group in a courtyard listening to a reading of the Bhāgavata-purāṇa from the lips of a demonstrative *guru*, who spoke the *çlokas* with much gesticulation and a peculiar unctuousness in the delivery of words like *Parameç-*

[1] See Fergusson's *Indian Architecture*, Appendix, and Oldenberg's Paper on Indian dates, translated in *Indian Antiquary*, x. (p. 268, foll.).

vara, that quite gave the effect of "the blessed word Mesopotamia." I fear there were not a dozen people in the town who could understand the Sanskrit of this work any more than the women and children who piously formed part of the congregation, and it is rather characteristic of a good deal of such religion, that the chance passer-by, who might have understood, was not allowed beyond the threshold.

My second day at Bhātgāon was partly occupied in photographing inscriptions and other objects. I also took a rough squeeze of the inscription of Yakshamalla noted above.

On this day I made some further efforts in my search for MSS., and my success was greater than I expected, but my negotiations were, I fear, interfered with by the officiousness of the Nepalese *mukhya,* or guard in attendance on me. As a general rule I had nothing to complain of in the demeanour of these men; on the contrary, on several occasions, so far from acting as spies or standing in the way of my investigations, they were of great use in overcoming the stupid prejudices against strangers manifested especially by the Buddhists of this country.

Nov. 26. After a day spent in work at MSS., with only short excursions, I made a third visit to Patan.

After photographing one of the inscriptions noted above, I explored as carefully as possible the western side of the town. Here, in a place called Puṃcaligāvāhār, I found a water-spout inscription bearing characters of the same period as those of the Mānadeva inscription noted above at p. 10. Both the dates however and the king's name are so far chipped away as to be, I fear, quite beyond recovery.

Not far from the same place I found a small tablet of slate dated N.S. 523 (A.D. 1403) and recording in Newari, mixed with Sanskrit, a religious donation "in the reign of the Yuvarāja Jayadharma-malla." In A.D. 1400 (*Catal.* Introd. p. ix. and table), we find from the colophon of our University Library MS. Add. 1664 a triple regency of Jayadharma with his two younger brothers: from this inscription it would seem that in 1403 Jayasthiti was still alive (as Jayadharma is called *yuvarāja*), but had abdicated at some time subsequent to A.D. 1392 in favour of his three sons; while subsequently the eldest superseded the other two in the regency. Finally in A.D. 1412 we find the second brother Jayajyoti[1] perhaps reigning alone. It is a curious illustration of the irregularity of the Nepalese chronicles that none of them, including that recently[2] commented on by Dr Bhagvānlāl Indrajī, make any mention of these three brothers, but agree in making Yakshamalla the son and immediate successor of Jayasthiti. Compare the revised table of kings of Nepal in Appendix III.

I proceeded next to photograph the picturesque tank known as Chāyavāhā. The Buddhist stūpa on the left bears inscriptions dated N.S. 577 and 579 (A.D. 1457—9).

The whole scene was selected as a favourable and characteristic specimen of the picturesqueness of the Nepalese town, showing as it does specimens of the tumular and pagoda styles of Nepalese religious architecture, and of the equally characteristic domestic work with carved wood fronts and overhanging eaves.

Nov. 27. On this day H. E. the Mahārāja kindly sent me a number of coins to examine. All with one exception were Nepalese silver of the XVIIth and XVIIIth centuries. I have noted a few dates and kings' names, not hitherto noticed, in my revised table of kings given below in Appendix III.

But the great event of this day was my visit to the Mahārāja's library. I did not, however, enter the room in which the books are usually kept, but the whole collection, consisting of many thousands of MSS., was brought for me from the palace to the Durbar-school building. So much trouble having been taken for my convenience, I made no enquiries as to the library room itself. Possibly the books are usually stored in one of those small rooms in which some of the best Indian collections of manuscripts (e.g. that in the splendid palace at Oodeypore)

[1] Catal. p. 155 ad fin.

[2] *Ind. Ant.* Dec. 1884, p. 414. In preparing this Report I have also made use of a MS. of the Vaṃçāvalī (acquired through Dr Wright by the British Museum), as far as my scanty knowledge of Hindi enabled me to verify statements from its crabbed dialect.

TANK WITH BUDDHIST CAITYA AND HINDU TEMPLE, CHĀYĀ-VAHĀ, PATAN.

Photographed by the Author.

are even now kept and which contrast so curiously with European ideas of a commodious library. If this be the case, we must hope that educational progress[1], now, we trust, commencing in Nepal, will extend to the affording of still greater and more regular facilities for the study of the unique literature of the country preserved in this collection of MSS., in many respects, as we shall see, the finest in India.

Several pandits were assembled to assist me, among them Ḍamaruvallabha Panta, known as a scholar beyond his native country and now teacher of Sanskrit in the *pāṭhsālā*. As to the obliging library-staff, I will only say that, however the books are *kept*, they are *found* with a quickness that many a European library cannot equal. As far as I know, I am the only European who has seen this collection, but some information as to its contents has on two occasions been placed in European hands.

One of these accounts is to be found in the lists sent to the University Library by Dr D. Wright, of which an abstract is given in my catalogue at p. 17: but I always understood that, so far from having seen the collection, he had doubts as to its existence; hence the remark there added, "It is impossible to say whether such a collection really exists," a statement which I am now glad to be able to reverse.

Another account is to be found in an official paper—like so many others, unknown to the few whom it might really benefit —kindly unearthed for my enlightenment by Mr A. Mackenzie, Home Secretary to the Government of India, at his office in Calcutta, during my subsequent visit to that place. It bears the somewhat strange title: "List of Sanskrit Works supposed by the Nepalese Pandits to be rare in the Nepalese Libraries at Khatmandoo." At the end occurs the subscription:

"R. Lawrence, Resident, Nepal Residency.
The 2nd of August, 1868."

[1] The very existence of the building in which I saw the books is a proof of this. Ten years ago (1875) Dr Wright wrote, "The subject of schools and colleges in Nepal may be treated as briefly as that of snakes in Ireland—there are none." Now we have at least one building in which both English and Sanskrit are taught, and, as I have every reason to believe, well taught.

That both this and Dr Wright's lists refer to the real collection seen by me, was proved by the classes of literature, which correspond exactly, in name and in number of books, with the rough but classified list of books which was first placed at my service at this visit to the library. There have been, however, very numerous accessions: nor can the rough list be anything like complete, for the MSS. in the library are counted not by hundreds merely, but by thousands.

I may add that I mentioned to H.E. the Mahārāja, a possible application for copies of works in the library, and found from the pandits in charge that the services of a copyist could be readily secured. I trust therefore that efforts will be made to obtain copies of some of the rare works which I now proceed to mention.

In Grammar (*vyākaraṇa*):

Library No.	Page in Lawrence's list.	
1558	9	*Cāndravyākaraṇa*, with commentary by Dharmadāsa. Palm-leaf; 159 leaves, 20 inches by 2; straight-topped character of XII.—XIII. cent., comparable to that of Add. 1648.

It would be of especial value to our library to obtain a copy of this fine MS., as we possess the only fragments of this grammar known to exist in Europe. My present acquisitions have all but completed the text, while we have several fragments of unidentified commentaries, which this MS. would put us in the way of assigning to their authors.

Library No.	Page in list.	
424	...	*Bhāshāvṛitti*, by Purushottama, with commentary called Bhāshāvṛittipañjikā by Viçvarūpa. Palm-leaf, Bengali writing.

I have remarked above, p. 13, on the rarity of the text. This commentary is, I believe, quite unknown.

I next give a list of plays, of which the first only appears in Lawrence's list:

1. Amṛitodaya nāṭaka.

2. Bhairavānanda, by Maṇika, produced under Rāja Jayasthiti (A.D. 1385—92). Compare our MS. Add. 1658 (Catal. p. 159).
3. Malayagandhinī.
4. Vidyātilaka.
5. Vimrālapana (?).
6. Çrīkhaṇḍacaritra.

None of these plays have been met with in India. I had unfortunately no time to examine them and to find how many were, like No. 2, local productions.

In *Jyotisha* (astronomy and astrology) I took notes of what seemed to me new, chiefly on behalf of Dr Thibaut of Benares, who is doing important work in this branch of literature. On my return to Benares I found that most of the works I had noted were unknown to him and to his accomplished astronomical pandit, Sudhākara Dube, of whom I shall speak later on. I may add that, though I can pretend to no special knowledge of the subject, so as to sift astronomical wheat from astrological chaff, I believe the works whose titles I subjoin to be of considerable rarity.

Library No.	Page in Lawrence.	
1459	11 also 3	Adbhutadarpaṇa.
1215	...	Jayacārya, by Narapati, with commentary (Jayalakshmī). Extracts from text only at Oxford (*Aufr. Cat.* 399 *b*).
1202	...	Mahāsaṅgrāmaratnakaraṇḍaka.
1196	...	Jayalakshmīsūryodaya. An old copy.
293	...	Saṃhitāvṛiti, by Meghapāla, 410 leaves.
1572	10	Nakshatramālā, by Jaganmohana.

Besides, I noted copies of the Rājamārtanda-jyotishapañjikā (No. 1210) and the Vasantarāja (No. 1011, an old copy) and the Horāsaṅkhyā (No. 1169), a part of the Toḍarānanda of Toḍaramalla. See Lawrence, p. 11, where also occur the titles of several other rare works. The collection having been formed, as I was told, by the late Sir Jung Bahādur, and thus probably collected by Hindu pandits, it was not to be expected that a large number of Buddhist works would be included; none indeed are mentioned in Lawrence's list; there is however a small number, and amongst them the following.

Library number.

772 Abhisamayālaṅkāra, a commentary on the Prajñāpāramitā, by Haricandra, 158 leaves, with 7 lines on a page, in the characteristic hooked character. Doubtless the same as the commentary at Calcutta. See Rājendralāl Mitra's Nepalese Buddhist Literature, p. 194, line 12.

This is a most important work, and a copy should certainly be asked for.

1103 Lokācārasaṅgraha. A collection of ritual books with Newari translation: paper, about 50 leaves.

772 (?) Bodhicaryāvatāra, followed by another work, 50 leaves, 12 × 2 inches, various Nepalese hands, XIII—XIVth cent.

My opportunity of examining this fine collection was only for the tantalising space of about four hours, for on the following day, when by this time I was just getting my arrangements for the acquisition of MSS. into good working order, I was obliged, owing to an intimation from the Resident given some days before, to leave the Government bungalow, which I had been occupying during my stay. The reason of this was an official visit from an officer of the Public Works Department. I regret extremely, on my own account and for those interested in my journey, that this circumstance should have put an abrupt end to my visit. Had I been fully aware of the conditions under which I resided in Nepal, I should have made negotiations (and these would have been, as I infer from subsequent experience, of a simple kind) for permission to occupy the tenement for a much longer time. As it was, I had no alternative but to leave the country[1].

[1] Mr Girdlestone had kindly arranged with the Durbar for a permit to visit two towns in the Tarai, both unknown to scientific travel; but the want of a pandit or native agent to accompany me decided me not to avail myself of this privilege. Should I be enabled to visit Nepal again, I have little doubt the pass could be renewed, and I should then make a point of securing the assistance of some person like my friend Pandit Bhagvānlāl. Is it too much to hope that the government of Nepal may some day see their way to do something in the cause of archæological research in their country, so rich in records of the past? We note with satisfaction that several of the more enlightened native states, like

I believe it will be seen from the foregoing pages that I found sufficient archæological work to keep me busily occupied during my brief stay. My collection of Buddhist and other MSS. acquired in Nepal more than realises my own expectations of the probable success of even a much longer stay.

The architectural studies which I had proposed to myself were almost entirely precluded by want of time. I had as a rule barely time to put down my notes of dates, etc., and on no occasion could I feel that time permitted the taking of measurements and accurate observation of details, to which Mr Fergusson refers in his work on Indian Architecture (p. 299 sqq.) as a great desideratum for the proper study of this interesting chapter of Oriental art-history.

After several days' uneventful journey I reached Calcutta, where my work was much helped by the friendly and scholarly kindness of Dr Hörnle and of Mr C. H. Tawney, formerly Fellow of Trinity College, to whom indeed, as already intimated in my preliminary Report, I am also indebted for help elsewhere in India.

Here no MSS. are to be had (so far as I know), except perhaps a few modern works from Orissa, of which I have brought one specimen. This is merely a Bhāgavata-purāṇa, which the owner, Mr L. J. K. Brace, Assistant Curator of the Botanical Gardens, desired me to present to the British Museum, in connection with certain botanical specimens of which I proceed to speak.

I visited the Botanic Garden of Calcutta—the most beautiful of the kind I ever saw—mainly to obtain dried specimens for the University Library of the various kinds of palm-leaf used for writing purposes, and these the same gentleman has kindly sent, and they are deposited in the library accordingly. I had never succeeded in obtaining very definite information on

Jeypore, have engaged in such work: and it is clear from the events at the great Rāwal-pindi durbar this year that Nepal no longer desires to pursue a policy of entire isolation from the current of civilization in India generally. I need hardly add that I should always be most willing and ready to avail myself of any practicable opportunity of personally directing or in any way furthering any scheme towards this end.

this point from botanical friends at home, but Pandit Umeçacandra Çarma, the courteous librarian of the Sanskrit College, Calcutta, pointed out to me that many of the best MSS. were written, not on the leaf of the common talipot palm (tālapattra), (Borassus flabelliformis), but on the more finely grained leaf of the *teret* (Corypha taliera and C. elata).

In the Calcutta Museum, the archæological part of which has recently been admirably arranged and catalogued by the Curator, Dr Anderson, I took copies of many of the unpublished inscriptions; but I understand that they will shortly be dealt with by Mr J. F. Fleet in his forthcoming volume on Gupta inscriptions.

As to the specimen of a hitherto unnoticed character, coinciding with the writing of a unique MS. fragment brought by me from Nepal, I may refer to my notes in Part II. § 2 below (Cāndravyākaraṇa). These are given in anticipation of a fuller study of this character, which I propose to publish hereafter, since, as far as I can judge at present, this discovery seems to be among the most interesting of my journey.

In the library of the Asiatic Society I examined the colophon of the oldest of the MSS. sent from Nepal by Mr Hodgson. As mentioned in one of the reviews (*Athenæum*, Jan. 5, 1884) of the Society's recently published catalogue of this collection, entitled *Nepalese Buddhist Literature*, some misapprehension seemed to exist as to the date of this MS. The results of my reading are given in Appendix III., in my supplemental table of kings of Nepal, where the date and king's name well accord with chronological results already established.

I also took advantage of my stay in Calcutta to read some portions of Sanskrit philosophical works, the full meaning of which is rarely understood by European scholars unless they have had the advantage of instruction derived directly or indirectly from the traditional school of interpretation in India. In this matter and in many others I have to acknowledge the very kind help of Professor Maheçacandra Nyāyaratna, Principal of the Government Sanskrit College. I was very glad to be able to call myself his *praçishya* (pupil's pupil). Perhaps in this iron age the *paramparā* (spiritual succession) can be passed on even through and to *mlecchas*; at any rate the best of brahmans could not have received kinder attention than I from the Professor and his pupil and assistant lecturer, Raghunāth Çāstri.

To the same friend and to another of his pupils, Bābū Haraprasāda Vandyopādhyāya, I am indebted for a most interesting afternoon spent in visiting two native schools for Sanskrit. A similar visit had been made two years before by Professor J. Jolly of Würzburg, who records his experiences most graphically in the *Deutsche Rundschau* for 1884[1]. The first of these schools is picturesquely situated on the Hooghly bank above Calcutta at Shamnagar. The building was given by the liberal Tagore (Ṭhākur) family, and, in spite of the doubtless sanctifying influence of *lingas* and shrines, shows, I regret to say, distinctly European influence in style.

Within, however, all is Oriental: not a chair in the place, except some kindly kept (I presume) for the infirmity of European visitors: teachers on the cushions surrounded by knots of pupils. In the highest class—that of the Nyāya philosophy—I found pupils of ages from fourteen to forty, some coming from distant parts of India. At the instance of Prof. Maheçacandra they had a disputation, much like one of our old Cambridge "Wrangles", in which was established, for my edification, after the rules of this philosophy, the existence of God.

To the next place, Bhātpāṛa, I was conducted by Bābū Haraprasāda, a collaborateur in Dr Rājendralāla Mitra's *Nepalese Buddhist Literature*, and met there by Bābū Hṛishikeça, both of them representatives of the few remaining old Bengali families who have for generations taken pride in endowing these simple seats of learning. It would be well, I think, for some disbelievers in Hindu disinterestedness, if they could see this body of venerable teachers, living in simple, dignified poverty, feeding as well as teaching their poorer pupils. How much in fact *is* known about such institutions by our Anglo-Indian friends, often so ready to generalize about the character of "the natives," may be estimated from the circumstance, that, though the place

[1] Bd. VII. of the *Halbmonatshefte*.

is only a few miles from the metropolis, I was (so I heard) only the third European who had ever visited it.

After a Christmas most pleasantly spent with Mr G. A. Grierson, joint compiler with my last host at Calcutta, Dr Hörnle, of the great work of a scientific Bihāri dictionary, I passed on to Benares.

On ground so well-trodden it might scarcely have been expected that any fresh archaeological discoveries would fall to my lot. Yet in a garden near the Raj Ghat I found a fragment of 10 lines in a character not later than the XIth century. As the stone was presented to me, I shall be able, when I have had leisure to examine it more carefully, to offer this, my single specimen of an original and not a mere copy of an inscription, to one of our University Museums.

The chief results of this second visit to Benares are to be found in my list of MSS. in Part II.

I also made some enquiries as to the Jain community of Benares. Owing to the kind introduction of the Raja Çivaprasāda C.S.I., himself a member of an old Jain family, I obtained access to the printing-press, and also to the library, connected with the Mandir, or Jain temple. The Maṇḍalācarya kindly had a transcript made, for my use, of his list of MSS., adding a promise to allow copies to be taken. This transcript I give in Appendix II., merely transliterating it and correcting a few obvious slips, but without attempting to verify the exact form of each title.

This library, not previously, I believe, visited by any European, may prove critically important to editors of Jain texts, as Jain MSS. are, as a rule, obtained from Western India. Though the community is of the Çvetāmbar sect, the library contains Digambar works also, e.g. the Kathākoça[1], of which I negotiated for a copy. This arrived in England shortly after I did.

[1] As there appear to be several collections of Jain tales with this general title, I may explain that the work referred to is that commencing with the story of Dhanada. Two tales from it have been printed by Prof. Nīlamaṇi Nyāyālaṅkāra in his Sāhityaparicaya from the Calcutta Sanskrit College MS., on which document the editor has, in more senses than one, 'left his mark.'

At the invitation of my friend Pandit Ḍhunḍhirāja Dharmādhikārī I attended a committee meeting of the new library started by the pandits of Benares, chiefly, I understand, at the suggestion of the pandit just named, in memory of the distinguished scholar Bāla Çāstrī, and called Bāla Sarasvatībhavana. The great feature of this library is that it is a place of deposit for MSS. on loan, not necessarily for good and all. If the very numerous owners of MSS. in the city can be induced only to deposit their books there, many of the characteristic risks incidental to their preservation in Indian houses will be avoided, and many rare books will doubtless come to light. At the same time, pandits are encouraged to bequeath works to the institution.

At the meeting[1] that I attended a scheme was also started for making search as to the contents of the private libraries of the city. It is indeed satisfactory, when one hears of difficulties placed in the way of the various Government officers in their search for MSS., to find here a body of native scholars willing not only to make known their own treasures, but to assist voluntarily and unofficially in the great work of literary search. One practical advantage of the institution to European scholars is, that it affords an opportunity of getting accurately made copies of almost any of the numerous works used by the pandits of Benares. Editors of philosophical texts especially may thus at once encourage a good institution and get an accurate copy by applying here.

As to the Government College Library, its present condition under Dr Thibaut and Pandit Sudhākar seems most flourishing. MSS. are constantly added, as far as the limited funds allowed by Government permit. It is however extremely unsatisfactory and discreditable to Benares to find that many of the works registered in Dr F. Hall's *Bibliographical Index* as belonging to this library 27 years ago are not now forthcoming.

A circumstance of this kind, occurring in the metropolis of

[1] I subsequently found an account of this meeting given in the Kavivacanasudhā, a Hindi journal of Benares for January 19th, 1885. My remarks on the occasion occupy a very unmeritedly large space, I fear, in the report.

Hindu learning and religion, ought to be borne in mind by all impartial persons in considering remarks like those of Dr Peterson at the end of his first Report on Sanskrit MSS. (1882—3, p. 72), directed against the sending of Sanskrit MSS. to Europe[1].

I had little time to spend in examination of the MSS. of the library, but amongst the philosophical books I noted the following as supplying information supplementary to that given by Hall.

(1) Two palm-leaf copies of the Nyāyalīlāvatī-prakāça, written in Upper Bengal in the years of the Lakshmaṇa era 389 and 395 (A.D. 1496 and 1501) respectively.

(2) The Nyāyavācaspati, a work of which I have not found any mention in Hall, or in any other work of reference, unless it be, as Prof. Cowell has suggested to me, the Nyāya-vārttika-tātparya-ṭikā (Hall, 21). Palm-leaf, Çaka 1531 (A.D. 1609).

(3) Kaṇādarahasya, an old copy acquired since Dr Hall's time.

(4) Praçastapadavācya (? °bhāshya), Çaka 1530 (A.D. 1608).

I trust that before long we may get a good catalogue of this important library, so that the world may be enlightened as to

[1] Dr Peterson will, I know, pardon me for adding a few words in self-defence as a collector for European libraries.

It seems to me that, without appealing to any national prejudices, which are out of place in questions of scholarship, a book is best kept wherever it is most safely and, in all senses, liberally kept.

As for the *safety* of MSS., every collector has his tale to tell of fine books packed away in roofs of houses, etc., and preyed on by damp and insects or other vermin. At all events the white ant has not yet been imported into our libraries.

As for *liberality in arrangement and description*, let me point out that, in spite of their advantages in respect of learned and helpful pandits, scholars in India, excepting Dr Rājendralāl Mitra and the late Dr Burnell, have given us nothing worthy of the name of a Catalogue.

Lastly as to *liberality in lending*, some Indian readers might well suppose in reading the above-cited passage that "sending to Europe" meant never coming back. Yet I am glad to be able to say that, while yet in India, I was the means of a well-known native Sanskritist's applying for and receiving a very ancient and valuable Sanskrit MS. from an English library.

the gains under the present excellent *régime*, as well as the losses since the appearance of Dr Hall's notes, which form so excellent a basis for the philosophical portion of such a compilation.

Besides much assistance generously rendered by Pandit Ḍhunḍhirāja, I received help in various ways from Dr Thibaut and Mr Venis of the Government College; also from Pandit Vindhyeçvarīprasāda, whose knowledge of bibliography is exceptionally wide; and from Pandits Lakshmīnārāyaṇa Kavi and Sudhākara Dube. The last named, who is the present librarian of the college, presented me with copies of several of his astronomical and mathematical works, written in Sanskrit. I am unfortunately not able to give an opinion on the scientific value of these, but I have deposited them in the University Library in the hope that they may be noticed, as I am informed by Dr Thibaut that Pandit Sudhākara is a mathematician of considerable originality, and that his researches deserve far more recognition than they have received, owing to his want of command of literary English. Dr Thibaut adds that he is willing to translate into English original papers by this pandit for reading before any suitable scientific society in Europe.

After some memorable days spent in Agra and its neighbourhood, I passed on to Jeypore.

Here I visited the very interesting library of H. H. the Mahārāja several times, permission—quite exceptional I believe in the absence of the prince—being most kindly granted me to visit it as often as I required. Some particulars as to this fine collection are to be found in Dr Peterson's first Report (1882—83). Much information will doubtless soon be at the disposal of scholars, as the work of cataloguing the collection is proceeding under the skilled hands of Lakshmīnātha Çāstri of Benares, assisted by Kṛishṇa Çāstri. Both of these pandits gave the most cordial help in my work at the library, and have been, I may add, in friendly communication with me since my return. In anticipation, I give a few notes on works that seem to be unique or otherwise remarkable. Under the subdivision of Rāmānuja philosophy, a school not much represented in libraries owing to its peculiar views as to the promulgation of its tenets, I found the following works.

Library marks.

1. *Vedārthasaṅgraha* by Rāmānuja, a MS. of 37 leaves; rare, but known to Hall, and quite recently printed at Madras in the Telugu character.

Darçana 942 and 3 2. A commentary on the preceding called *Vedārthasaṅgrahatātparya-dīpikā* by Sudarçana Sūri, who is known as a commentator on Rāmānuja's Çrībhāshya. The present commentary has, I believe, not been hitherto met with.

3. *Tattvamuktākalāpa* by Venkaṭācārya, sometimes called Venkaṭanātha. Can this be the work cited in the Sarvadarçana-sangraha (see Cowell and Gough's translation, p. 86, note)?

In *Jyotisha* I noted:

Jyotish 45.3 4. *Rājamṛigāṅka* by Bhojadeva, a personage to whom several works in various branches of literature are attributed. This copy was made in Çaka 1450 (A. D. 1528) by Jyotirvid Çrīdatta son of Saṅka (?) आत्मपठनार्थं

In dramatic literature I noted a couple of local productions:

Kāvya 36.15 5. *Janakīrāghava-nāṭaka*, attributed to the *Yuvarāj* Rāmasiṃha, son of Jayasiṃha, who was reigning about A.D. 1625. MS. written A.D. 1664.

Kāvya 37.13 6. *Prabhāvalī*, a play in four acts, composed by Harijīvana Miçra at the command of the said Rāmasiṃha when *rāja*.

I may also mention:

37.8 7. *Hāsāmṛita*, a farce composed by Viṭṭhalakṛishṇa Vidyāvāgīça at the command of Sujanasiṃha, described as reigning in Bandelkhand; 16 leaves.

8. *Pārthaparākrama*, a *vyāyoga* in about 500 *çlokas*, by a *yuvarāj* called Prahlāda. This is followed by the beginning of a play called

9. *Dūtāṅgada* by Rāmachandra.

I noted next two pandits' plays, written on the model of the Prabodhacandrodaya, and intended to illustrate philosophy:

Kāvya 37.5 10. *Svanubhūti-nāṭaka* by Ananta Paṇḍita son of Tryambaka. Various schools are discussed. 63 leaves.

37.1 11. *Kṛishṇabhakticandrikā* by Anantadeva, author of the Smṛitikaustubha, who flourished at the beginning of the XVIIth cent.

12. *Ghṛitakulyā*, a farce in about 250 *çlokas*. MS. dated V. S. 1731 (A.D. 1674).

The above with the exception of No. 11 (as to which see Bühler, Cat. MSS. in Gujarat II. 116) are, I believe, unknown.

I noted also two copies of the

37.6 59.2 13. *Laṭakamelana* by Çaṅkhadhara, a farce apparently satirising the Digambara Jains, who however speak ordinary dramatic Prākṛit. Dr Bühler (*Cat. Guj.* II. 122), and also Dr Peterson in his second Report (for 1883—4) note copies of this.

I visited of course, as all travellers do, the ruined city of Amber, the former capital of the state. At a place so much in the track of visitors I scarcely expected to find anything of fresh archæological interest, but it is a characteristic proof of the amount of quite elementary work still remaining to be done in Indian Archæology, that, in a small, though not ruined, Temple of the Sun overlooking the town I found a short inscription bearing a date nearly half a century earlier than anything hitherto known in connexion with the place. See Appendix I.

I will add here a suggestion made by my kind host Dr T. M. Hendley, who was my guide on this occasion, that the fine 'Jagatsohana' temple in this ruined town might give many most useful hints to the architects of Christian churches in India. Indeed not only the main buildings, but the whole precincts present a strong and curious analogy to an ecclesiastico-collegiate establishment.

According to my custom of visiting schools where Sanskrit is still taught on the traditional plan, I went to H. H. the Mahārāja's Sanskrit *Pāṭhsālā*, where I was kindly received and shown round by Pandits Rāmbhaja and Çivarām. Everything, as far as one can judge, seems progressing favourably on the old lines.

During my stay at Jeypore, I had the pleasure of many interviews with Pandit Durgāprasāda, whose knowledge and appreciation of literature are most exceptionally wide.

I next spent a day or two at Ajmere, where I copied the large XIIth century Sanskrit inscription carefully preserved in the famous Aṛhāī-din-ka Jhopra. Strangely enough, it seems to be still unpublished.

Hence I passed on to Nimbahera, whence Col. Walter, Resident at Oodeypore, had kindly arranged a *ḍāk* for me to Oodeypore.

In this city, in situation the most beautiful[1] perhaps in India, I spent a short time, without however achieving any of the success in the matter of MSS. gained by Dr Peterson some years before. I attribute this to my want of an agent. Dr Peterson had sent on his native assistants previously, and they no doubt materially prepared the way for him. Should I visit India again, I should make a point of securing the services of some pandit to assist me in this way.

In archæology, however, I found at Oodeypore many matters of interest; and here I was most materially helped by Bābū Çyāmal Dās, Kavirāj (court poet or herald) to H. H. the Mahārāṇa. My courteous host Col. Walter had kindly informed him of my approaching visit and its purposes, and the Kavirāj lost no time in extending to me the right hand of fellowship.

I proceed to give a short account of the literary work, a very important one in my opinion, on which the Kavirāj is engaged. The chief families of Rajputana have usually employed a herald or family bard, who has in some sort chronicled their deeds. Bābū Çyāmal Dās has made a most fitting use of his position as royal herald in causing these to be collected and having digests made of their contents. From these, and from the general chronicles and royal *vaṃçāvalīs*, which are extant for the state of Oodeypore (or Meywar), the

[1] See the glowing, yet not too enthusiastic description in L. Rousselet's "*L'Inde des Rajahs*" (p. 174), and the still more eloquent words of Dr Peterson (First Report, pp. 48—50), embodied in one of those footnotes which I have also supposed the strictly literary traveller may sometimes allow himself.

VII.

TEMPLE NEAR THE PALACE, OODEYPORE.

Photographed by the Author.

Kavirāj is compiling a history of this state. I was much surprised to find in his library a very fine collection of books in all the chief European languages, bearing on the history and topography of Rajputana. Bearing in mind, however, how much history and panegyric run into one another in Eastern literature, it is most important to find that, supplementing his work, is a systematically collected series of inscriptions, which exist in such numbers in these parts. The growing interest (though still it is surprisingly small) felt by native scholars in their own ancient monuments and the records they bear, is one of the encouraging sides of the influence of Western thought in India, though one must confess that Europeans may still do much to make up for the influences, so deteriorating in many ways, which they and their civilization have brought to bear on native morality and native art.

But to resume. By the direction of my kind friend I was guided to several spots interesting both for architecture and inscriptions. My guide was Pandit Rāmpratāp, who has worked specially for the inscription section of the forthcoming history. The pandit is in the employment of the Durbar, and his services both here and later at Chittor were kindly placed at my disposal by H. H. the Maharāṇa, with whom I had more than one interview, at which he manifested a most friendly interest in the objects of my visit.

I visited of course the celebrated royal cemetery, the Mahāsatī, as to which Mr Fergusson[1] remarks: "All [the tombs] are crowned by domes and all make more or less pretensions to architectural beauty; while as they are grouped together as accident dictated and interspersed with noble trees, it would be difficult to point to a more beautiful cemetery anywhere." Possibly the place has been somewhat neglected since Mr Fergusson wrote; at present the beautiful and varied effect of the architecture is seriously marred by the weeds and undergrowth, and by the want of suitable paths. Outside the precincts of the cemetery proper I was shewn by the pandit several smaller tombs, which he told me were those of ministers

[1] *History of Indian Architecture*, p. 471.

of the state. Several of these are evidently of considerable age and merit attention.

Not far from this is the village of Aṛ or Ahaṛ, abounding in objects of archæological interest, which have never been properly described. There are several Jain temples, not all of them at present in use. In one I noted an interesting series of shrines built round the square lower end of a temple courtyard. These were later additions and in almost every case bore the name of the donor and date of erection, the dates being mostly of the XIVth century. Some of the images contained in them, however, if not the buildings themselves, were of earlier date. I noted one fine undraped figure of a Tīrthaṃkara or Jain 'apostle' bearing date [Vikrama] Saṃvat 1031 (A. D. 974). Just outside one corner of the temple wall and on a lower level, so as to be partially excavated, were cells in which the monks formerly resided. Many of these have short inscriptions in Prākṛit, and bear dates chiefly of the XVIth century of the Vikrama era.

Besides the Jain temples we find in Aṛ traces of forms of cult a little removed from the ordinary run of Hindu temple worship. In a temple close by that just described I noted a shrine of a Nāga or serpent, which I think is of somewhat rare occurrence in modern India. The image was four or five feet high and was erected in the XVIIth century.

The next record is that of sun-worship, comparatively rare, as already observed, and little studied or scientifically understood in India. I found here no temple of the sun, as at Amber (p. 29), but a fragment of an inscription, from which it would appear that in the reign of Çaktikumāra (X—XIth cent.) the previously existing practice of offering each year 14 *drammas* (δραχμαί) of some oblation to the sun was formally confirmed. This inscription may serve as another instance of the large amount of archæological work still to be done in India. I discovered it on a piece of marble built into some steps leading to the terrace where stands the Jain temple just described. Here it had escaped the notice of my excellent guide Pandit Rāmpratāp, though he was evidently familiar with these little visited temples and their inscriptions.

The Pandit has sent me quite recently, too late indeed for me to publish it, as he kindly desired, in the present work, a beautifully executed squeeze and transcript of another inscription discovered by him since my visit in the same locality and containing mention of the same king.

The fine Sanskrit library of the palace, where I was most kindly received by my friend the Kavirāj and a number of pandits assembled in my honour, calls for no description from me, as Dr Peterson's "Detailed Report for 1882—83," an extra number of the Bombay Asiatic Society's Journal, is in the hands of all scholars. In the library catalogue, which will, I trust, during the present reign be amplified and ultimately printed, I noted a small work of a few lines only on a strange subdivision of Çilpa-çāstra, the construction of beds, certainly very late, as the (xvth century) Vāstu-maṇḍana is quoted. It seemed to me of some interest to find an addition to this division of literature (constructive art), always so thinly represented in Indian libraries, composed at so late a date in the classical language, and a copy was kindly presented to me, which I keep as a souvenir of my visit and also to help in affording material for studies in this little-studied branch of literature, which I hope to prosecute when I have leisure.

I was now permitted to visit the ruins of the ancient city-fortress of Chittor in the same state, the scene and often the very centre of Rājpūt and Musulman warfare for so many centuries. Here again I profited by the excellent guidance of Pandit Rāmpratāp, who had spent three months on the spot copying the very numerous inscriptions bearing on Rājpūt history, and doubtless also searching for fresh ones under the piles of ruins on every side.

I observed with regret that the tree noticed by Major H. H. Cole in his first *Report on Ancient Monuments* (p. clxxxii), as growing on the top of the older of the towers of Victory, was still unremoved. Not far from the famous tower of Khumbo Rāṇa, and above the tank called by Major Cole the *gau mukh*, is a cave, which has apparently been used as a Jain hermitage. In it are several Prākrit inscriptions, in characters that appear to be of about the XIVth century. I have copies of several, and should they turn out interesting I shall publish them before long. To have made a detailed study of them just now would, with the unfortunately very limited amount of *daylight* leisure at my command, have delayed the present publication too long.

My stay in Chittor was limited to a part of a day, and I could not but feel with some regret what a field for historical, archæological and artistic discovery I was leaving in the state of Meywar, both here and nearer the capital. It is certainly strange that more work of this kind has not been done hereabouts. The Government of India, which has of late manifested practical interest in archæological research, certainly seems hitherto to have been rarely successful in gaining the services of officers at once qualified to criticize the artistic and constructive details of ancient buildings and to interpret and digest the documentary evidence, both literary and monumental, connected with them.

Passing hence to Indore, I endeavoured, in this instance without success, to prosecute my work of collecting MSS. A short visit to the ancient city of Ujjain, or rather to the very modern representative of the old city, proved also unavailing. So far from finding traces of the ancient astronomical learning for which the town was once renowned, I found the pandits scarcely conversant, it would seem, even with the names of the chief works on the subject.

As my allotted time of absence was now drawing to a close, I returned to Bombay, where I met by appointment Pandit Bhagvān Dās, who has long been the energetic agent of the Bombay Government for the collection of Sanskrit MSS. By a minute of this Government the agent is allowed to sell duplicates of works in the Government collections for the use of certain institutions in this country, of which our University Library is one. A rough list of the fine collection that I purchased from him is given in Part II. § 1.

I left Bombay for Europe on March 1st.

Thus terminated a tour which, if it has not resulted in any

literary or archæological discoveries of first-rate importance,—such as can only be reasonably looked for in the work of travellers of greater experience and leisure,—may nevertheless, I believe, be held to have justified the grounds of my application to the University in respect of the Worts Fund.

There now only remains to me the pleasing duty of acknowledging the sympathy and assistance I have received from various quarters. In referring first, as becomes me in the present work, to the liberality of the University, as manifested in the grant from the fund just named, I wish particularly to testify to the great encouragement I received not only from the benefaction itself, but from the generous conditions under which it was bestowed. The only condition in fact was the preparation of a Report,—a provision which the present work is designed to fulfil; and in view of the friendly and unsparing way in which the Syndics of our University Press have met my wishes as to its publication, I may say that this very condition has been turned into an additional privilege.

I venture thus to call attention to the circumstances under which I worked for the University, not because I would imply that to those acquainted with the history of the English Universities such treatment will seem at all exceptional, but because I feel bound to bear witness, which many fellow-workers can confirm, to the great stimulus to exertion afforded by such frank confidence, unhampered by the cramping restrictions by which scholarship amongst us, when encouraged at all, is too often hindered.

My project of travelling so many thousands of miles, and buying everything of literary value to me on my way, which seemed a somewhat ambitious one, was also encouraged and furthered by the very kind and timely assistance of two friends, Professor Cowell and the Reverend A. J. Harvey, M.A., of St. James's, Paddington.

Owing to the great kindness and hospitality of the residents in almost every part of India that I visited, my journey was unexpectedly attended with so little expense that I had no occasion to avail myself of the funds lent by these friends for the purchase of MSS., but my obligation, and indirectly I may perhaps add, that of the University, is none the less.

The names of many friends and fellow-scholars in India, who so kindly entertained and in every way assisted me, will have been met with in the foregoing pages; nor would it have been so necessary to dwell on their kindness but for the recent publication of the rather crude 'ideas' of an English traveller, which I found had produced a most unpleasant effect upon the various societies that had done their best to receive him cordially; and, I must add, doubtless did an amount of mischief among the natives that the writer could perhaps hardly realize[1].

[1] I say mischief: for, although the paper (since separately published under the title 'Ideas about India') contains many true and forcible remarks (or, it may be, random shots that occasionally hit the mark), and this may be very salutary reading for some Anglo-Indians, or even for Englishmen at home, if other more thorough books be read in connexion, yet to native readers the whole tone will be most misleading.

As to the passage in Mr W. Scawen Blunt's first paper (*Fortnightly Review*, Vol. XXXVI., p. 175), alluded to in the text, on the luxury of Anglo-Indians, which has given more offence perhaps than any other, if it be appropriate that one cold-weather tourist should rebuke another, I would remind Mr Blunt that it is, to say the least, not always cool in India, and that things that may rank as luxuries here become necessaries of healthy life there. Many of Mr Blunt's most extraordinary statements seem to me simple cases of hasty generalization, which even my own limited observation serves entirely to correct. So far from having found that "no Collector's wife will wear an article of Indian manufacture, to save her soul from perdition" ('Ideas,' p. 29), I got from several kind hostesses many valuable details about Indian clothes and ornaments, which I found that they not only wore themselves but also sent home to their friends in Europe. So far from Englishwomen looking on "the land of their exile as a house of bondage," I have generally found ladies at home preserving the kindest recollections of their Indian life, not excluding the relations with their native servants and dependents. For these, be it observed, are the only natives with whom, as a rule, our countrywomen *can* have much to do, not so much owing to prejudices on their side (though these often doubtless exist), but rather to the barbarous and un-Aryan practice forced upon the Hindus (properly so called) by the ancestors of Mr Blunt's Muhammadan friends. In fact, in those parts of India where Muhammadan rule chiefly prevailed, very few of even the best natives have been at all educated up to the *ideal* of the society of ladies, and for *this* reason, which seems to have escaped Mr Blunt's notice, free social intercourse is out of the question. As a contrast alike to the real average native of a region such as Upper Bengal, and to Mr Blunt's supposed typical Anglo-Indian lady (*ibid.* p. 47), it is a pleasure to me to be able to cite the testimony of an English

But I hope that European residents in India will understand that scholars at least, who start with no preconceived social or political 'ideas' to be proved, can accept the ungrudgingly rendered assistance of their fellow-subjects of every race, without turning it to a root of bitterness and unmerited reproach.

The great kindness shown to me by native scholars has, I trust, been made evident by what I have said in this Report. It was indeed most encouraging to find what a bond of union is formed by enthusiasm for a common study between races sometimes supposed to be almost by nature unblending or even antagonistic. I had not, indeed, expected to find any hostility to my work on the part of the pandits, but in the place of the shy reserve, which even some European scholars accustomed to work like mine had led me to expect, I was often quite surprised at the cordiality and frankness with which both Hindus and Jains came forward to help me. Nor did my native friends and helpers proffer their assistance simply while I was present to ask it, *κατ' ὀφθαλμοδουλίαν ὡς ἀνθρωπάρεσκοι*; on the contrary, I have received since my return MSS., books and copies of inscriptions from several places that I visited, and scarcely a mail has arrived without bringing me letters from my Indian friends.

To each and all of them, who may chance to read these pages, I can only say, in recording my thanks, that I trust we may meet again before very long, whether some of them may be induced to visit Europe during 1886 from the double attraction of specially Indian celebrations in London and Vienna, or whether I may be permitted to utilise the knowledge and experience I have been gaining by again visiting India.

With such a hope let me conclude. As I have stated in my

lady, the wife of a well-known scholar, who has travelled in many parts of *Western* India amongst the manly Rājputs and the Mahrattas, that she has never met with anything but courtesy from native gentlemen, and that in entertaining, as she often does, the younger members especially of the various higher castes and nationalities (for, *pace* some popular writers and talkers, there is no such thing as '*the* Indian people'), she considers their manners even superior to those of the corresponding age and class in Europe.

preliminary Report[1], the results described in the foregoing pages need only be regarded, so far as the University is concerned, as a beginning: and for myself I feel that the time and energy which circumstances may leave at my disposal for scholarly work cannot be better employed than in working out at home the material for research thus obtained, in the hope of some day supplementing it by fresh work in the same distant yet pleasant fields.

[1] See the *Cambridge University Reporter* for May 26, 1885, p. 736. Whether used much by myself or by other Sanskritists at Cambridge, I will hope that students in other places will avail themselves of my collection. For (if I may be allowed to repeat an observation made in the preface to my Catalogue of our Buddhist MSS.) the tendency of recent so-called reform has been practically to discourage the prolonged residence in the University of those of its members whose special literary pursuits cannot at once be utilised for the conduct of the ordinary round of its studies; and I fear that it will be some time before Prākṛit is studied at our universities in the same way as the Greek and Italian dialects, and perhaps still longer before we may hope for what is already found in some foreign universities, the systematic *comparative* study of religion and philosophy.

PART II.

LISTS OF MSS., WITH NOTES.

I NOW proceed to give an account of what formed the chief object of my journey, the search for MSS.

I therefore give (§ 1) lists of the MSS. collected by myself and of those collected by Pandit Bhagvān Dās and bought together from him, as mentioned above (p. 34).

Of my own MSS., about 212 in number, I have made a classified list. For the Pandit's collection of nearly 300 MSS., I have contented myself with transliterating the very rough list drawn up by or for him. I have corrected a few obvious slips, but I have not had time to verify all names or add dates of writing etc. from the MSS. themselves.

All these, with the exception of a few marked with an asterisk, are now placed at the disposal of the University on terms explained in a Report addressed to the Library Syndicate.

Notes are given (§ 2) on some of the chief MSS. in my own collection. I could have wished, as I have already intimated in the preface, that these could have been fuller and more comprehensive. But I trust that the MSS. may be properly catalogued, along with the valuable collection of Jain MSS. acquired by the University some years ago.

I also give (§ 3) notes on MSS. in India, copies of which might advantageously be negotiated for.

§ 1. CLASSIFIED LIST OF MSS. PERSONALLY COLLECTED.

CONTENTS.

ABBREVIATIONS.

B. MSS. acquired in Benares and the North-West Provinces.
N. " Nepal.
R. " Rājputāna.

* An asterisk, as above stated, indicates that the MS. is reserved and not sent to the University Library.

Note. Except where otherwise stated, all MSS. from Nepal are on palm-leaf, and the rest on paper.

MSS. are arranged under their titles.

The dates of writing are put in the equivalent years of the Christian era.

I. VEDA.

(α) *Saṃhitā.*

Anuvākas, collection of. B.

Bhāshya by Uäta on the Ṛikprātiçākhya.

(β) *Brāhmaṇa.*

Çatapatha-brāhmaṇa.—Madhyama-kāṇḍa. 1528. *Imperfect.* B.

Çatapatha-brāhmaṇa.—Hasti-k°. 1582. B.

Taittirīya brāhmaṇa (?), fragm. B.

Vārttika-sāra. B.

(γ) *Sūtra.*

Āpastambīya-sūtra. A *prayoga-vṛitti* connected with Dhūrta-svāmī's comm. on the A°.; *Praçnas* 1, 2, and part of 3. B.

Pāraskāra-gṛihya-sūtras. I.—II. 8, xvth cent. palm-leaf, the remainder xviith cent. paper. Wanting 6 lines at end. N.

Paribhāshā. B.

Pavamānahoma-prayoga. 1786. B.

Piṇḍapitṛiyajña-vyatishaṅga by Raghunātha Vājapeyi. 1635. B.

Prāyaçcitta-dīpikā. 1787. B.

Sautrāmaṇi-prayoga. 1786. B.

(δ) *Upanishads.*

Aitareya-upanishad, Çaṅkara's comm. on, 1593. B.

Anubhūtiprakāça (metrical version of the Upanishads) by Vidyāraṇya-svāmī (Sāyaṇa). B.

Bṛihadāraṇyaka-up°. A gloss on Çaṅkara's comm. B.
Chāndogya-up°. 1517. B.
„ (another copy). 1772. B.
Māṇḍūkya-up°. : Ānandagiri's gloss on Çaṅkara. B.

II. Purāṇa.

Agnipurāṇa. N.
Bhāgavata [one skandha] Bengali hand. N.
Çivagīta. B.
Çivapurāṇa followed by Çivadharmottara, xith cent. N.
Skanda-p°.—Kedāra-khaṇḍa. 1649. Beng. hand. N. Paper.
Vishṇupurāṇa. Beng. hand of xv—xvith cent. N.
Vṛishasārasaṅgraha. B (?).

III. Itihāsa (Epic).

Mahābhārata: Sabhāparvan. 1693. N.
„ Udyoga-p°: Sanatsujātīya with Çaṅkara's comm. B (?).
Rāmāyaṇa.—Āraṇya-kāṇḍa. 1652. N.

IV. Kāvya (Belles lettres).

(a) *Kāvya.*

Bhaṭṭi: Sargas I—XIII., with comm. (not Jayamaṇgala's or Bharatamallika's); Sargas IV—V. Mostly xvth cent. N.

Meghadūta, with Sarasvatītīrtha's comm. called Vidvadbālarañjinī.

Meghadūta with anonymous commentary. Kashmiri-Nāgari writing.

Sāraṅgasāratattva, circa 1690. B.

(β) *Nāṭaka.*

Anargharāghava (?). Fragm. of 3 leaves. Beng. hand, xv—xvith cent. N.

Çṛiṅgāravāṭikā by Viçvanātha. B.

Ekādaçīvrata-nāṭaka, *circa* A.D. 1480. N.

Mahāvīracarita. *Imperf.* xvi—xviith cent. (?). B.

Mudrārākshasa. 1376. N.

(γ) *Campū.*

Damayantīkathā (or Nalacampū) by Trivikramabhaṭṭa. 1628. R.

Damayantīkathāvṛitti (comm.), begun by Candrapāla and finished by Guṇavinayagaṇi. 1853. R.

(δ) *Kathā.*

Hitopadeça [N.S. 493 A.D.] 1373. N.

*Mādhavānalopākhyāna. 1751. N. Paper.

Siṃhāsanadvātriṃçikā; Jain hand (Jain recension?) 1606. R.

*Tantrākhyāna. 1485. N.

V. VYĀKARAṆA (Grammar).

Bhāshyapradīpoddyota. Supercommentary by Nāgojibhaṭṭa on the Mahābhāshya. B.

Cāndravyākaraṇa. See Buddhist works, below, XI.

Dhātupārāyaṇa by Pūrṇacandra. N.

*Kāraka-kaumudī. R.

Prabodhacandrikā by Vaijala. 1857. B.

Samāsavāda by Jayarāma. B.

*Sūtras with comm. not identified. N.

VI. CHANDAḤ AND ALAṄKĀRA (Metrica and ars poetica).

Alaṅkāratilaka or Kavyānuçāsanavṛitti by Vāgbhaṭa.

Devīstotra of Yaçaskara (Çārada character). B.

Prākṛita-piṅgala. (Part of the Piṅgala-çāstra). R.

Rasamañjarī by Bhānumiçra with Gopālabhaṭṭa's comm., Rasikarañjanī. 1837. B.

Vāgbhaṭālaṅkāra with (new) comm. 1467. R.

VII. JYOTISHA (Astronomy and astrology).

Bālavivekinī with comm. by Nāhnika. 1823. B.

*Tājikasāra by Haribhadra Sūri. 1404. R.

Trivikrama-çata. R.

VIII. DHARMAÇĀSTRA (Law).

Brāhmaṇasarvasva by Halāyudha. B.

Çuddhiviveka by Rudradhara. 1789. R.

Çukranīti. Ch. I. 1851. R.

Kālamādhavīya (fragment). B.

*Nārada-smṛiti with Newari version, and fragments of Newari works. N.

Rājadharmakaustubha, part of Anantadeva's Smṛitikaustubha. B.

IX. Art.

(α) *Vaidya* (medicine).
Bhīmavinoda (?). *Imperfect.* N.
(β) *Çilpa* (constructive art).
*Prasādamaṇḍana by Maṇḍana.
*Viçvakarmaprakāça. B.
(γ) *Kāma* (ars amoris).
Anaṅgaraṅga by Kalyāṇamalla. 1614. R.
Ratimañjarī by Jayadeva. R.
*Vātsyāyana with comm. N.

X. Darçana (Philosophy).

(α) General.
Sarvadarçana-saṅgraha. B.
Khaṇḍanoddhāra, supercommentary by Pragalbha Miçra on Harsha's Khaṇḍana-khaṇḍa-khādya.
(β) [*Sāṅkhya* and] *Yoga*.
Haṭhasaṅketacandrikā by Sundara. *Imperf.* 1831. B.
Yogasūtra with Bhoja's comm. *Imperf.* B.
Yogavāsishṭasāra with Mahīdhara's comm. B?
(γ) *Nyāya* and *Vaiçeshika*.
Anyathākhyāti-vicāra (or °-vāda) [by Timmaṇṇa]. B.
Bādhabuddhivāda by Harirāma Tarkavāgīça. B.
Dīdhiti-māthurī (cp. Māthurī below). Pt. of § ii. only. Comm. on Tattva-cintāmaṇi. *Imperf.* B.
'Gaurīkāntī' Gaurīkānta's comm. on Keçava's Tarkabhāshā. B. *Imperf.*
*'Gaurīkāntī' (another copy)? complete. B.
(Vaiçeshika) Guṇakiraṇāvalī-prakāça by Vardhamāna. Wants ff. 1—7. B.
Kiraṇāvalī (?) (Fragment). B.
Māthurī. Comm. by Mathuranātha on Tattvacintāmaṇi. (Part of Khaṇḍa 1 only). Beng. hand XVII—XVIII cent. B. *Imperf.*
Nirukti. Comm. on Tarkasaṅgraha. Telugu character. ? perfect. B.
Nyāyasiddhāntamañjarī 1760.
Ratnakoshavāda (?). Defective at end. B.

Saptapadārthī, 1625. R.
Sārasaṅgraha. Comm. on Tārkikarakshā by Varadarāja. Ch. I. B.
Tarkaprakāçikā. Comm. by Çitikaṇṭha on Bhaṭṭacārya-cūdāmaṇi's Nyāyasiddhāntamañjarī. 1760. R.
Tātparyavādavicāra. B.
Yogyatāvicāra. B.

(δ) *Vedānta* [and *Mīmāṃsā*].

Advaitasiddhi by Madhusūdana Sūri. B.
Advaitasiddhi, commentary by Brahmānanda. B.
Aparokshānubhūti. Comm. on Çaṅkara's work. B.
*Aparokshānubhūti (another copy). B.
Ātmapurāṇa by Çaṅkarānanda; wanting Ch. 9. 1726. B.
Çrutisāra by Toṭaka with comm. by Saccidānanda Yogi.
Çukāshṭaka with comm. by Gaṅgādharendra Sarasvatī. B.
Gītātātparyabodhinī by Ānandasarasvatī. B.
Jñānasvaprakāça. B.
Kaivalyakalpadruma by Gangādhara Sarasvatī. B.
*Nyāya-makaranda and its ṭīkā (or vivṛiti) by Citsukha Muni. Text by Ānandabodha. Kashmiri-Nāgarī character. 1841. B.
Praçnāvalī by Jadubharata. B.
Pañcadaçī III. IV. with Rāmakṛishṇa's Comm. B.
" (another copy) I—III. V. B.
Sañjñāprakriyā. B.
Siddhāntaleçasaṅgraha. (End of last chapter wanting). B.
" (commentary) defective at end. B.
Siddhāntavindu by Madhusūdana, a comm. on the Daçaçlokī B. (?)
Svarūpanirṇaya by Sadānanda. B.
Svātmanirūpaṇa by Çaṅkara, with 'Aryā'-vyākhyā by Saccidānanda Sarasvatī. B.
Tattvānusandhāna by Mahādevasarasvatī. B.
Tattvapradīpikā ("Citsukhī"). Jain hand of XVI—XVIIth cent. B.
Upadeçasahasrī with comm. B.
Vairāgyataraṅga. B.
Vākyavṛitti-prakāçikā, comm. on Çaṅkara's Vākya-vṛitti. B.
* " (another copy). B.

Vedānta-kalpataru. B.

Vivekacūḍāmaṇi by Çaṅkara. 1815. B.

A collection of short Vedantic treatises [called Mahāvākyaprabodha (?)]. B.

XI. Buddhist works. (All from Nepal.)

[1]Ashṭasāhasrikā-prajñāpāramitā. c. A.D. 1020.

" (another copy).

Cāndravyākaraṇa I—II § ii. and part of II § iii., with comm. differing from that of Add. 1657. 1

*Cāndravyākaraṇa...§ 5, 6. In an unknown character.

Kāraṇḍavyūha (prose version). Illuminated. 1196.

Lalitavistara. As to date see notes in Report. } Paper.

" (another copy). 1684. (The oldest copy known.) }

*Pañcarakshā. Palm-leaf (modified Kuṭila writing) with modern paper supply. Dated in reign of Vigrahapāla of Bengal (c. 1080).

Pañcarakshā (another copy). Archaic hand with more recent supply.

[2]Saddharmapuṇḍarīka. 1093. With last leaf of another work dated 1065.

Vasudhārā-dhāraṇī. xvth cent.

Fragment of prayers, rituals etc., xivth cent.

XII. Jain works. (All from Rājputāna.)

(a) *Canonical.*

§ i. *Aṅgas and Upāṅgas.*

Anuttaraupapātikā with Sanskrit glosses.

Prajñāpanā (Paññā°). V.S. 1521 (A.D. 1464).

§ ii. *Other canonical works.*

Aürapaccākkhāṇa; see below under Saṃstāra.

Āvaçyaka-laghuvṛitti: pratikramaṇa-section.

Āvaçyaka. 1534.

Daçavaikālikā with avacūri (A.D. 1400).

[1] Lent to Dr Rājendralāla Mitra: deposited at Bengal Asiatic Society, Calcutta.

[2] Lent to Dr Hörnle: deposited at Bengal Asiatic Society.

*Daçavaikālikā (text only). 1469.
Daçaçrutaskandha. § 8. Paryushaṇākalpa (Padyosavaṇa-kappo) 1521.
„ (another copy). A.D. 1760.
Piṇḍaniryukti.
{Saṃstara followed by
{Atura- (Aüra-) pratyākhyāna.
Vyavahāra with comm. A.D. 1708.
Another work called Paccākhāṇa (pratyākhyāna).

(β) *Extra-canonical treatises etc.*

Añjanāsundarī-Yavanakumārasambandha. 1657.
Anyokti.
Bandhasāmitta : see below, Shaṭsūtra.
Çataka „ „ „
*Çāntināthacaritra.
Çīlopadeçamālā.
Çrāvakāṇām mukhavastrikā-rajohāraṇavicāra. 1597.
Çrāvaka-pratikramaṇa.
Chandonuçāsana.
Dharmasaṅgraha by Medhāvin. (*Imperfect.*)
Dīpotsava.
Dravyasaṅgraha by Nemicandra.
Gotamakulaka.
Guṇavarmacaritra (Pūjādhikāra).
*Harivaṃça-purāṇa.
Jīvasamāsa with Çīlācārya's comm.
Jīvavicāra (by Çāntisāra).
Kālakācārya-kathā.
„ „ (another copy with glosses). A.D. 1840.
*Kalpāntarvācya (by Ratnacandratilaka) 1638; with vernacular fragments; one dated 1672.
Kalyāṇamandira by Siddhasena. With comm.
Karmastava. } See Shaṭsūtra.
Karmavipāka. }
Kathākoça (Vrata-Kathāk°).
* „ „ (another collection; v. supra, p. 24).
Laghukshetrasamāsa-vṛitti by Haribhadra. A.D. 1434.
Lumpāka-mata-kuṭṭana.
Meghanāda-madanamañjarī-kathā. 1552.

Navatattvaprakaraṇa. 1695.
Nemi-purāṇa. 1776.
Pradyumna-carita by Somakīrti.
Pramāṇa-nirṇaya.
Praçnottara ratnamālā with comm.
Ṛishimaṇḍala. 1549.
Sādharaṇajina-stavana by Jayānanda, with comm. 1658.
Sāmbodhipañcāçikā. 1736.
Saṃyaktvakaumudī. 1695.
Saptatikā }
Shaḍaçīti } : see below Shaṭsūtra.
Shaḍāvaçyaka with *bālabodha.*
Shaṭsūtra : the six works are :

1. Karmavipāka (Kammavibāga).
2. Bandhasāmitta.
3. Karmastava.
4. Shaḍaçīti.
5. Çataka.
6. Saptatikā.

Shaṭsūtra (another copy) with comm. on No. 5 and 6.
„ Commentaries on Nos. 1—4.
Sindūraprakaraṇa. 1843.
„ (another copy with comm.)
Stotras to Çāntinātha and others. 1698.
Upadeçamālā.
Upadeçarasāla by Sādhuraṅga. 1599.
Vāgbhaṭālaṅkāra. See *Alaṅkāra.*
Vicāramañjarī.
*Vicārasāra.
Vicārashaṭtriṃçikā. 1854.
Vivekamañjarī by Āsaḍa.
Yati-ārādhana-vidhi.
Yogaçāstra, comm. by Jinameḍana, pupil of Somasundara.
Several Paṭṭāvalīs.
A treatise by Somasundara, ff. 4, 64 verses.

XII. TANTRA, RITUALS, AND MISCELLANEOUS WORKS.

Kāraṇḍavyūha : see Buddhist works. N.

Trivikramasundarī or Jñānadīpavimarshiṇī. N.
Anonymous Çivaic work. XIIIth cent. N.
Bhuvaneçvarīstotra by Pṛithvīdhara with Padmanābha's comm. 1733. R.

ROUGH LIST OF MSS. PURCHASED AT BOMBAY.

Jain MSS.

1. Abhayadeva's comm. on the Antakṛiddaçā.
2. Siddhasena's comm. on the Pravacanasāroddhāra.
3. Abhayadeva's comm. on the Bhagavatisūtra.
4. Abhayadeva's comm. on the Vipāka.
5. Nirayāvalī.
6. Sthānāṅga.
7. Jñātādharmakathā.
8. Uvavāī (Abhayadeva's comm.)
9. Daçavaikālikā.
10. Upadeçamālā.
11. Uttarādhyayana.
12. Ākhyāta-avacūri.
13. Sūtrakṛita.
14. Siṃhāsanadvātriṃçikā (? Jain recension).
15. Kumārasambhava.
16. Padyosavaṇakappa (Paryushaṇā).
17. Rājapraçnīyam.
18. Uttarādhyayana-avacūri.
19. Liṅgānuçāsana-avacūri.
20. Jīvābhigama.
21. Sūryaprajñapti.
22. Padyosavaṇa with *ṭippaṇi*.
23. Praçnavyakaraṇa with Abhayadeva's comm.
24. Piṇḍa...avacūri.
25. Yogaçāstra.
26. Çāntinātha-caritra.
27. Ācārāṅga.
28. Daçavaikālika.
29. Malayagiri's comm. on Rājapraçnīya.
30. Abhayadeva's comm. on Upāsakadaça.
31. Āvaçyaka-avacūri.
32. Pushpamālā.
33. Antakṛiddaçā with comm.
34. Jñātādharmakathā.
35. Sūtrakṛita (niryukti).
36. Kalpasūtra-avacūri.
37. Abhidhānacintāmaṇi of Hemacandra.
38. Laghu-saṅgrahaṇī-ratna.
39. Bhagavatī.
40. Kalpa-kiraṇāvalī.
41. Pārçvanāthacaritra.
42. Jīvābhigama.
43. Pākshika.
44. Vallabhadeva's comm. on Kumāra-sambhava.
45. Abhayadeva's comm. on Jñātādharma-kathā.
46. Ārādhana-sūtra.
47. Pratikramaṇa-sūtra.
48. Yogaçāstra.
49. Jambudvīpaprajñapti.
50. Abhidhānacintāmaṇi comm.
51. Antakṛiddaçā.

52. Kshetrasamāsa.
53. Ṛishimaṇḍala.
54. Dhātupāṭha with comm.
55. Oghaniryukti.
56. Kalyāṇamandira with comm.
57. Anuttaraupapātika.
58. Kalpāntarvācyāni (A.D. 1457).
59. Prajñāpanā.
60. Prauḍhamanorama.
61. Çabdānuçāsana (imperf.)
62. Varāhī saṃhitā (part only).
63. Çabdānuçāsana, pt. 2. (Saṃv. 1482).
64. Çabdānuçāsana, pt. 8.
65. Lingānuçāsana (Hemacandra)
66. Çabdānuçāsana, pt. 4.
67. „ pt. 2 (2 leaves wanting).
68. Çabdāvacūrṇi pt. 1.
69. „ pt. 2.
70. Çabdānuçāsana pt....?
71. „ pt. 1.
72. „ pt. 5.
73. „ pt....?
74. „ pt....?
75. Ākhyātāvacūrṇi.
76. Prajñāpanā with comm.
77. Dharmabuddhi-kathā (?).
78. Āturapratyākhyāna.
79. Taṇḍula-vaiyālika.
80. Sūktamuktāvalī-ṭīkā.
81. Samavāyāṅga.
82. Candraprajñapti.
83. Vītarāgastotra.
84. Çabdānuçāsaṇa-vṛitti, pts. 1 and 2.
85. Kalpāntarvācyāni (cf. 58).
86. Āvaçyaka.
87. Sarvajanopadeça.
88. Laghusaṅgrahaṇī with comm.
89. Bhavabhāvanā (Hemacandra).
90. Paramātmaprakāça.
91. Shaḍdarçanasaṅgraha.
92. Kriyākalāpa.
93. Jambudvīpasaṅgrahaṇī with comm.
*94. Rohiṇī-Açokanṛipa-kathā.
95. Çrāddha-pratikramaṇa-sūtra-vṛitti.
96. Munipaticarita.
97. Dhātupāṭha.
98. Navatattva.
99. [Tales.]
100. Çabdānuçāsana, comm. (Part of Adhy. V.).
101. Yogaçāstra.
102. Ācārāṅga-sūtra-vṛitti (Çīlāṅgāchārya).
103. Pratyākhyāna-bhāshya.
104. Saṃyaktvakaumudī.
105. Shashṭi-çataka.
106. Kshetrasamāsa-avacūri.
107. Āvaçyaka-avacūri.
108. Pratyākhyāna-bhāshya with avacūri.
*109. Kūrmaputra-kathā.
110. Adhyātmasāra.
111. Vidagdhamukhamaṇḍana-ṭīkā.
112. Vicārashaṭtriṃçikā.
113. Sthirāvalī.
114. Guṇasthānavivaraṇa.
*115. Gurvāvali with comm.
116. Dravyasaṅgraha.

117. Gautama-pṛicchā.
118. Saṅgrahaṇī with comm.
119. Çabdānuçāsana (Adhy. V.).
120. Shaḍāvaçyaka.
121. Jambūcaritra (with praçasti, slightly imperfect).
122. Divālīkalpa (?).
123. Çabdānuçāsana (Adhy. III).
124. Saptatisthāna.
*125. Campakaçreshṭhi-kathā.
*126. Maunaikādaçī-māhātmya.
127. Vipāka sūtra.
128. Kālakācārya-kathā.
129. Āvaçyaka-niryukti-ṭīkā.
130. Navatattva with comm.
131. Nandī-vṛitti.
132. Anekārthasaṅgraha with comm.; *imperfect.*
*133. Sambodha-sattarikā.
134. Bhaktāmara with comm.
135. Anushṭhānasubodha (*imperf.*).
136. Samācārīçataka.
137. Trishashṭiçatakapurusha-caritra (part of).
138. Khaṇḍapraçasti.
139. Pratyākhyāna-niryukti.
140. Jñānārṇavayogapradīpa.

Brahmanical and general MSS.

141. Narapati-jayacaryā.
142. A collection of Upanishads.
143. Vṛitabadha-paddhāti.
144. Vedānta-paribhāshā.
145. Tājika-sāra.
146. Anekārthadhvani-mañjarī.
147. Prabodhacandrodaya.
148. Holāshṭaka.
149. Siddhāntamuktāvalī.
150. Strījātaka.
151. Vedāntasāra.
152. Bhuvanadīpaka.
153. Nīlakaṇṭha-tājika.
154. Smṛitisārasamuccaya (*imperf.*)
155. Kaivalyopanishad.
156. Pratishṭhā° kalanirṇaya.
157. Dhātupāṭha.
158. Makarandāharaṇa.
159. Praçna-vaishṇava.
160. Bhojaprabandha.
161. Bṛihaj-jātaka.
162. Ramalacintāmaṇī.
163. Tājikapaddhati with comm.
164. Sarvasaṅgraha.
165. Uāta-bhāshya (*imperf.*)
166. Raghuvaṃça-comm.
167. Sārasvata, Mādhava-ṭikā.
168. Çāradātilaka (*imperf.*)
169. Ghaṭapartha-kāvya.
170. Dhātupāṭha.
171. Gaṅgā-pīyūshalaharī.
172. Pratishṭhāmayūkha.
173. Vākyasudhā.
174. Laghujātaka.
175. Ajapāgāyatrī.
176. Jātakapaddhati.
177. Ramalapraçna.
178. Upākarmapaddhati.
179. Nighaṇṭu.
180. Rasamañjarī.
181. Makaranda-ṭippaṇa.
182. Siddhānta-muktāvalī.
183. Çriṅgāratilaka with comm.
184. Vasishṭha-çānti (Saṃv. 1510).
185. Pratyaṅgira-kavaca.

186. Rasamañjarī.
187. Caraṇavyūha.
188. Asaucanirṇaya.
189. Pañcaviveka.
190. Vaidyamanorama.
191. Triçatī by Çārṅgadhara.
192. Ashṭavakra with comm.
193. Amaranāmamālā.
194. Bhārata-tilaka.
195. Parāçara-smriti.
196. Vetālapañcaviṃçati.
197. Vishṇusahasra-nāma-bhāshya.
198. Ācārādarça.
199. Indraprasthamāhātmya.
200. Brahmasūtra.
201. Prāyaçcitta-mayūkha.
202. Çrāddha-mayūkha.
203. Vishṇu-purāṇa.
204. Naishadha - commentary (Çāradā character).
205. Ghaṭakarpara with comm.
206. Makaranda-vivaraṇa.
207. Nyāya-siddhāntamañjari.
208. Pāṇini's Ashṭādhyāyī (from Kashmir).
209. Kuvalayānanda, comm.
209a. Garuḍopanishad-dīpikā (Kashmir).
209b. Amarakosha (Çāradā character).
210. Hemādri, Pariçesha-khaṇḍa (imperf.).
211. Veda racārtha (?) (Çāradā).
212. Jñānārṇava (*imperf.*).
213. Çabdabodha.
214. Vṛihad-naradīya-purāṇa (unfinished).
215. Anekārtha-mañjarī.
216. Māgha-durghaṭa.
217. Yājñavalkya-comm. (*imp.*).
218. Durghaṭa-kāvya with comm.
219. Lagnabrāhmaṇa (60 çlokas).
220. Arthavivecana.
221. Mahimna-stotra with comm.
222. Rudrabhāshya (Çāradā).
223. Laghukaumudī (Çāradā, *imperf.*).
224. Āçvalāyana-gṛihyasūtra.
225. Kaularahasya.
226. Lalita-paramarahasya (Çāradā).
227. Kāvya-subhāshita.
228. Sambandha-viveka.
229. Rājamārtaṇḍa (*imperf.*).
230. Nilotsarga-vidhi (*imperf.*).
231. Mātṛikā-nighaṇṭu.
232. Dharmopastava-khaṇḍana by Vedāntavāgīça Ācārya.
233. Grahaçānti.
234. Mīmāṃsā-rahasya (one adhyāya only).
235. Siddhānta-candrikā.
236. Ashṭavakra-comm.
237. Amarakosha-comm.
238. Çārṅgadhara (medical).
239. Pañcadaçī (with comm.)
240. Suçruta.
241. Chāndogya-upanishadvivaraṇa (*imperf.*).
242. Anuvāka.
243. Yogārṇava.
244. Nyāya-çāstra.
245. Nirṇayasindhu.

246. Jātakābharaṇa.
247. Vājasaneyī.
248. Vṛihaj-jātaka.
249. Çaṭacaṇḍī-paddhati.
250. Mṛityuñjaya-japavidhi (*imperf.*).
251. Cintāmaṇi comm.
252. Rasarāja.
253. Vīramitrodaya, comm.
254. Pasakakevalī (?).
255. Muhūrtacintāmaṇi, comm.
256. Cāturmāsyavṛita.
257. Nītimayūkha.
258. Çrāddhaviveka.
259. Mahimna with comm.
260. Nāciketa-upākhyāna.
261. Muhūrtamārtaṇḍa.
262. Raghuvaṃça.
263. Laghusiddhāntakaumudī.
264. Vishṇubhaktikalpalatā.
265. Nyāyamañjarī.
266. Kumārārtha-vivecana by Ekanātha.
267. Rāmakṛishṇavilāpa-kāvya.
268. Mahārudra-paddhati.
269. Nāgara-khanda (*imperf.*).
270. Punarārādhana-nimittāni.
271. Kaiyyata's comm. on the Mahābhāshya.
272. Māgha-kāvya, comm.
273. Sāmavedasaṃhitā (*imp.*).
274. Cāṇakya (*imp.*).
275. Jātaka-paddhati with comm.
276. Çīghrabodha.
277. Vṛittaratnākara, comm.
278. Muktāvalī-prakāça.
279. Samara-sāra.
280. Kāvya-prakāça (*imperf.*).
281. Ṭabba-cintāmaṇi (?).
282. Çatapatha-brāhmaṇa (fragment of 1000 çlokas).
283. Rasāyana-tantra.
284. Āçvalāyana-brāhmaṇa (?).
285. Jātakakarma-paddhati.
286. Çatapatha-brāhmaṇa (850 çlokas).
287. Yogaçataka.
288. Tulasī-vivāha.
289. Yogavāsishṭha (fr. of 400 çlokas).
290. Vāradarājīya-vyākhyāna (*imperf.*).
291. Jyotishaçlokāḥ (500 çl.).
292. Gītagovinda.
293. Muhūrtamārtaṇḍa.
294. Çabdakaustubha.

§ 2. NOTES ON PARTICULAR MSS. ACQUIRED.

(1) From Nepal.

I regret that I have little of fresh interest in Buddhist literature. There will be found however several fresh MSS. of works already known, as well as several non-Buddhistic works of some importance.

Cāndra-vyākaraṇa. Several new fragments.

A partial exception may be noted in the case of the *Cāndra-vyākaraṇa* or grammar of the Cāndra school of grammarians, attributed to Candragomin, a Buddhist author. Of the text and its commentaries our library already possesses several portions, which are duly noted in the Catalogue.

I have now secured several new fragments of this work.

The first of these (List, XI, 4) has the great interest of being written in a character unknown to me and, I may say, unknown in India also, for I showed the MS. or a specimen of the character to all the chief authorities in such matters, both European and native, in Northern India.

In the Calcutta Museum however I observed a figure of Buddha on a pedestal inscribed with characters somewhat more difficult to decipher than those of my MS. (indeed I learned from the Curator that the inscription never had been read), but still bearing the same distinguishing feature: namely, a triangular ornament at the top of each vertical stroke in the letters. The form of letter with thick tops tapering down into a quasi-triangular form is well known, but here we get the apex of the triangle uppermost. Besides this there are many very curious archaisms in the letters themselves.

I have obtained a photograph of the figure above-mentioned, and with the help of this and of my squeezes and rubbings I hope to be able to publish a complete study of this character before long.

Parāsara-gṛihya-sūtra. Vedic texts seem to be rare in Nepal. There seems to be little of consequence in this literature even in the great Durbar library. The owner of the present MS. evidently had no idea of what it was, as he described the book in a list that he sent to me simply as '*choṭā-wālā*' "little one." Parāsara-gṛihya-sūtra.

Mahābhārata.—Sabhāparvan. This MS. is remarkable as being by far the latest Nepalese palm-leaf I have met with. The colophon records that it was written "for the hearing [*i.e.* so that the book might be read to] King Yoganarendra Malla, by the Bengali Brahman Harihara in Nepal saṃvat 813 (A.D. 1693)." Mahābhārata.

Hitopadeça and *Mudrārākshasa.* These books were written by the same scribe at an interval of three years, N.S. 493—6 (A.D. 1373—6). It is I think of some importance for the history of the Hitopadeça, which has usually been regarded as a somewhat late redaction of the great collection of the Pañca-tantra, to find that in the middle of the XIVth century it had already gained enough celebrity to be copied in the valley of Nepal. Hitopadeça and Mudrārākshasa.

I also acquired a large MS. which was stated by its owner to be the Bhīmavinoda. Unfortunately, the book is imperfect at both ends, and I can find no clue to its name in any chapter-title; nor could I get any assistance in recognising the work from various pandits to whom I showed it in other parts of India. Part of an index remains. This begins with the treatment of special diseases (*jvarātīsāra* 'fever and dysentery' fol. 66 of original MS.) and ends with various general modes of treatment (*dhūmapāna — kavaḍa — nasyādi* "smoke-inhaling, rinsing, sternutatories" ff. 528—531). A large fragment of a medical work said to be the Bhīmavinoda.

I obtained another copy of the *Tantrākhyāna*, a work already in the Wright collection. It is a collection of tales, of which many, but not all, occur in the Pañca-tantra and Hitopadeça. The work deserves investigation in connexion with the studies in Indian folk-lore now in progress in several quarters. It consists of 43 short stories, chiefly in verse. The Tantrākhyāna.

first is of the tortoise and the two geese; the second, the prince and the ape.

In the same covers, and written by the same scribe 'Jasa'-varmā, is a quasi-dramatic piece on the *Ekādaçī-vrata* or the vow of the eleventh day, composed (fol. 4, *a* 4) for king Jaya-ratna Malla.

Tripura-sundarī of Vidyā-nanda-nātha.

The *Tripurasundarā-paddhati* or *Jñānadīpavimarshiṇī* is an unknown Sivaic ritual-book by an unknown author, Vidyā-nandanātha or °nāthadeva, described as *Mahāpadmavana-shaṇḍa-vihārī.* A full alphabet is given on f. 74 *b*.

Anony-mous work.

Another work is remarkable as being by far the smallest palmleaf MS. yet found in Nepal, as it measures only $5 \times 1\frac{1}{2}$ inches. It has no title and I have not succeeded in identifying it. It is divided into 28 *adhyāyas,* and commences with a dialogue between Çiva and Parvatī.

Nārada.

I now give some extracts from a very full description kindly supplied to me by Professor Jolly of Würzburg of a fragment obtained by me in Nepal, which has turned out to be a new recension of the Nārada-smṛiti. My discovery of this MS. has been most opportune, as he is at present printing a critical edition of the text as a fitting sequel to his valuable translation of this *dharma-çāstra.*

The first portion of the MS.

"The Nepalese MS. of the Nārada-smṛiti is very valuable indeed, both on account of its marked divergence from all the other MSS. of that work, that have come to light hitherto, and on account of its age. It is dated, at the end, N. S. 527, whereas none of the other MSS. is more than a hundred years old. The first portion of the Nepalese Nārada has apparently been lost and supplanted by fragments of two different works in the Nepalese language, the first of which extends from fol. 1 to fol. 24*a*, and is written in a very clear hand. It is described at the end as a Nepalese commentary on a Nyāyaçāstra (*iti nīnāmakṛitanyāyaçāstranepālabhāshāṭipini samāptaḥ*), and dated 527, like the fragment of Nārada. Fol. 24 *b* and fol. 27 (25 and 26 are missing), seem to contain fragments of another

Nepalese composition. They are very badly written. The fragment of the Nārada-smṛiti, accompanied by a commentary in Nevari, is written in yet another hand, and begins at fol. 28 *a* with the words: *vṛittir eshā dāreshu guruputre tathaiva ca* ||, which correspond to the latter portion of paragr. 8, V. Head of Dispute, in the Indian MSS., and in my English translation of the Institutes of Nārada. The following leaves, up to fol. 93, agree in the main with the Indian recension, as contained in my translation and in the edition which I am printing, from seven Indian MSS., in the *Bibliotheca Indica*." Nārada.

[Prof. Jolly here subjoins a most valuable list of various readings, which I omit as being beyond the scope of the present work, and also because I trust his edition will shortly appear.]

"It will be seen from the list of various readings that the Nepalese MS. is a valuable check on the Indian MSS. of Nārada. In many cases, the superior correctness of its readings admits of direct proof through the numerous quotations from the Nārada-smṛiti, which are scattered through the Mitāksharā, Vīramitrodaya, and other Commentaries and Digests of Law. It is true that in a number of other cases the quotations speak in favour of the readings preserved in the Indian recension of Nārada. The Nepalese MS. is also by no means free from serious blunders. Character of the above-mentioned readings.

"The last Vivādapada, called Prakīrṇaka, does not however constitute the final chapter of the Nepalese, as it does of the Indian, Nārada. It is followed, first, at fol. 93 *b*, by a long chapter on Theft or Caurapratishedha, as it is called in the colophon (*nāradaproktāyāṃ caurapratishedhaṃ nāma prakaraṇaṃ samāptam*). The opening çlokas of this chapter agree very closely with Manu IX. 256—260. The remainder has its counterpart both in Manu IX. 252—293, and in the eighth chapter of the Code of Manu, where the subject of Theft is treated at considerable length (VIII. 301—343). It may seem strange that an additional chapter on Theft should thus be introduced at the close of the whole work, after all the eighteen Vivādapadas have been discussed in their order. Precisely the same want of consistency is, however, observable in Manu's An additional chapter on Theft.

treatment of forensic law, a chapter on Theft and kindred matters being tacked on, at the close of the section on forensic law, in the Code of Manu as well as in the present text. This fact goes far to prove the genuineness of the chapter on Theft in the Nepalese MS. It is also important, because it gives fresh support to the truth of the traditional statements, which connect the composition of the Nārada-smṛiti with the Code of Manu. Indian tradition is wrong, it is true, in making the Nārada-smṛiti an early recension of the Code of Manu. The chapter on Theft, as well as the entire previous portion of the book, is full of detailed rules and provisions, which are decidedly less archaic than the corresponding rules of Manu. It consists of no less than 61 çlokas and one trishṭubh. Moreover, it contains a reference to a coin called *dīnāra*, which corresponds to the Latin *denarius*[1]. Some texts from this chapter are expressly attributed to Nārada in the Vīramitrodaya.

The final chapter on Ordeals. "It is more difficult to account for the addition, at fol. 106 *b* of the Nepalese MS., of a final chapter on Ordeals, which subject is usually treated in the law of evidence.

The end. "At fol. 118 *a* the whole work closes as follows: idam alpadhiyāṃ nṛiṇāṃ durvijñeyaṃ yathoditam | nāradīyaṃ yad astīha nyāyaçāstraṃ mahārthavat || tasyeyaṃ likhyate ṭīkā spashṭā nepālabhāshayā | imāṃ vijñāya bhūpādyāç carantu nyāyavartmanā || ° || iti mānave nyāyaçāstre nāradaproktāyāṃ saṃhitāyāṃ nyāyadharmapadāni samāptāni || ৩ || saṃvat 527 kārttikamāse, etc. The last clause, which contains the date, is written in different hand from the remainder of the work, and very indistinctly. The colophon, in accordance with some of the previous colophons, describes the work of Nārada as a recension of the Code of Manu. This tends to confirm the Indian tradition, above referred to, regarding the connexion of Manu with Nārada. See, too, my *Tagore Law Lectures*, pp. 46 and 57. It is curious that the Code of Manu is called a Nyāyaçāstra in the last colophon. The term *nyāya* in this compound is no

[1] Regarding the occurrence of this term in the previous portion of the Nārada-smṛiti, see West and Bühler's *Digest of Hindu Law*, 3rd ed., p. 48 and Jolly, *Tagore Law Lectures* (Calcutta 1885, Thacker and Spink), p. 56.

doubt an equivalent for *dharma*, as is not seldom the case in the law-books, e.g. Nārada XVII. 9. The same use of the term recurs in the two çlokas just quoted, in which the author of the Nepalese Commentary declares that he has written it for the enlightenment of kings and others, as the Nārada-smṛiti is difficult for the ignorant to understand."

(2) GENERAL COLLECTION (Benares, Rajputana, etc.).
Kāvya (Poetry, etc.).

Though six commentaries on the Meghadūta are made known to us by Aufrecht (*Bodl. Catal.* p. 125), I have acquired two copies of the text with commentaries hitherto, as far as I know, unnoticed. Two Commentaries on the Meghadūta.

The MSS. give the text in somewhat different forms, as the first has 122 distichs and the second 113, while the Oxford copy above cited has 116. Two of the spurious verses noted by Aufrecht (आनन्दोत्थं and आश्वस्यैनां, here given as आश्वस्यैवं,) occur in the first MS. as vv. 71 and 118 respectively. The commentary to this MS., called Vidvadbālānurañjinī, was written at Benares by Sarasvatītīrtha, called in the commentary itself 'Yati' and in the colophon 'Paramahaṃsa Parivrājakācārya.'

In the second MS. the name of the commentator is not given in the colophon. He thus refers to himself and his work in verses 2 and 3:

कालिदासवचः कुत्र व्याख्यातारो वयं क्व च ।
तदिदं मंददीपेन राजवेश्मप्रकाशनं ॥
तथापि क्रियतेऽस्माभिर्मेघदूतस्य पंचका ।
उन्नताश्रयमाहात्म्यस्वरूपख्यातिलालसैः ॥

This MS. is written in the fine bold form of Nāgari for which the scribes of Kashmir are celebrated. An antique Kashmirian form of घ may be noted in leaf 1 line 4, in the third of the lines just quoted. Several other good examples of this writing, besides one instance[1] of the old Kashmirian or Çāradā, may be found in the present collection. In the Jeypore royal library I found one Kashmirian copyist at work.

Māgha-durghaṭa.

À propos of commentaries on the *Kāvyas* I may call attention in passing (though this is included in the collection of MSS. from Bombay [No. 216] which I am not able at present to describe) to a collection of short adversaria on the Māgha-kāvya called *Māgha-durghata*, by one Rājakrūḍa.

Sāraṅga-sāra-tattva.

Sāraṅgasāratattva. This is a collection of 200 verses on polity or general morality. In spite of the strange form of the title it would seem to be compiled from the Çārṅgadhara-paddhati. The last clause runs: माकन्दादिव मञ्जरी घनभरावर्षवया निर्गता सेयं शार्ङ्गधरात्तनोतु जगतां चेतोमुदं पद्धतिः । Though obtained at Benares, the MS. was written for the Maharāṇa Jayasiṃha, who reigned at Oodeypore A.D. 1680—99.

Nala-campū, comm.

In the special form of poetical composition called *campū*, I obtained a MS. of a *ṭippaṇa* or commentary on the Damayantīkathā or Nala-campū by two Jains, Candapāla and Guṇavinaya Gaṇi, with a paṭṭāvalī of these commentators.

Nāṭaka (Drama).

Çriṅgāra-vāṭikā.

Under this head I have a portion of a play, the *Çriṅgāra-vāṭikā*, or 'love-garden,' produced for Vishṇusiṃha, *Kumāra* of the Mahārāja Rāmasiṃha, doubtless the sovereign of Jeypore, whom we noticed above (p. 28), as a patron of the drama. Of the 29 remaining leaves (for the leaf numbered 30, placed with the rest, does not belong to this MS.), 10 are occupied with the prologue, from which we learn (f. 5 *a*) that the story tells of Candraketu son of Vijayaketu, king of Avantī, who left his kingdom to the care of his minister Buddhisāgara and travelled to Campāvatī. The first scene discovers him with his companion, the Vidūshaka; his adventures are described in the garden of Kāntimatī daughter of Ratnapāla, king of that city (f. 15 *a*—*b*).

[1] This is a copy of the *Devistotra* of Yaçaskara; see p. 43 above, Sect. VI.

Alaṅkāra (Rhetoric and *ars poetica*).

Under this head we have a copy of the *Vāgbhaṭālaṅkāra* with an anonymous commentary not previously, I think, noticed. Vāgbhaṭa with comm. In it we find Vāgbhaṭa called by a Prakritized form of name, Bāhaḍa or Bāhaḍadeva. The subscription of Chapter IV. runs: इति बाहडमंत्रीश्वरविरचितवाग्भटालंकारे चतुर्थः परिच्छेदः and in the final subscription the author is styled मंत्रि वाग्भट; so that we may perhaps infer that he was the minister of the king Jayasiṃha (cf. Aufrecht, *Bodleian Catalogue*, 214 *a*), under whom the work was composed. The commentator identifies this king with the son of Karṇadeva cited by Aufrecht.

The MS., which is a good specimen of Jain calligraphy, was written in V.S. 1524 (A.D. 1467) during the pontificate of Lakshmīsāgara of the Tapāgaccha, who attained his *sūripada* in V.S. 1508 (see Klatt in *Ind. Ant.* XI. 256).

I have also obtained a copy of the *Alaṅkāratilaka* (cf. Alaṅkāra tilaka. Bühler, *Cat. MSS. Gujarat*, III. 44). A second title of the book is *Kāvyānuçāsana*. This is likewise the work of a Vāgbhaṭa, who from the introduction is clearly a Jain and in the postscript is described as famed for 'the composition of several new works' (नव्यानेक महाप्रबन्धरचना). He may thus be fairly identified with the author of the Vāgbhaṭālaṅkāra; but being also described as the son of Nemīkumāra, he must be separated[1] from the medical Vāgbhaṭa, who was the son of Siṃhagupta and named after his grandfather Vāgbhaṭa[2].

A third work among my few, but on the whole interesting, Rasa-mañjarī with comm. specimens of Alaṅkāra-literature is Bhānudatta's *Rasamañjarī* with a commentary called Rasikarañjanī by Gopāla Bhaṭṭa, son of Harivaṃça Bhaṭṭa. This MS. supports the reading विदेहभूः, noticed by Professor Rāmkrishṇa Bhāṇḍārkar (Report on Sk.

[1] In spite of the tradition referred to by Burnell, *Cat. Tanjore*, 57 *b*.

[2] See the verse quoted from the physician's own writings by Anna Moreçvara Kunte in the preface (p. 6) to his edition of the Ashṭāṅgahṛidaya, which may be taken in modification of Prof. Aufrecht's statement that Vāgbhaṭa's parentage is 'subscriptionibus tantum librorum traditum' (*Cat. Bodl.* p. 303, not.).

MSS. 1882—3) as giving the right indication of the author's birth-place.

Darçana (Philosophy).

Various Vedantic works.

Praçnāvalī, by Jadubharata, pupil of Mādhavānanda; a catechism of Vedantic doctrine.

Svarūpanirṇaya a Vedāntic work on the nature of *ātman* by Sadānanda, clearly the same as that mentioned by Hall (*Index*, p. 129) though this copy has about 2000 çlokas as compared with 800 in Hall's. My MS. has four chapters (*pariccheda*), the last being entitled *jīvanmuktibhūmikānirūpaṇa*.

Svātmanirūpaṇa by Çaṅkarācārya. The commentary by Saccidānanda Sarasvatī, which is mentioned without any special name by Hall (p. 104), is given, and styled Āryā-vyākhyā.

Çrutisāra, by Toṭakācārya, said to have been a pupil of Çaṅkara. The only other known copy of this work seems to be a MS. at Tanjore (Burnell, p. 95 *a*). The work consists of 160 çlokas; and our MS. has a commentary by Saccidānanda Yogi, 'Yogīndra-çishya,' of which I have found no trace elsewhere.

The *Saṃjñāprakriyā* is a short compendium of Vedantic terminology which may prove useful to the lexicographer as well as to the student of philosophy. I have not found mention of the work in any catalogue of MSS.

The *Gītātātparyabodhinī* is a Vedantic commentary on the Bhagavadgītā by Ānandasarasvatī, an author of whom nothing appears to be known. The present MS. contains *adhyāyas* I. II. VII. VIII. and part of IX.

Jain works.

Sambodhi-pañcāsikā. This is a tract of 50 verses in Prakrit on *saṃsāra*, the *dharma* and other teachings of Jainism, in the form of instruction given to a pupil by the author, Gotama Svāmī. Each verse is accompanied by a paraphrase in Sanskrit.

It would be interesting to know why we find in the text the month, in the commentary the month and day, but in neither the year, when the book was composed.

Dharma-saṅgraha.

Dharmasaṅgraha. This is a work in verse on various religious topics by Medhāvin, who describes himself as Çrī-Jinacandrānte-vāsī. In Ch. I. verse 6 we find a reference to श्रीजिनसेनकः..कर्त्ता महापुराणस्य. After some verses on cosmogony the chapter concludes with a legend of king Çreṇika, its title being 'Çreṇikānandavarṇana.' At f. 11 are some descriptions of the architecture and decorations of shrines.

Pramāṇa-nirṇaya.

The *Pramāṇanirṇaya* is a discussion of the various kinds of *pramāṇa*, or sources of knowledge, after the manner of the ordinary philosophical works. The chief divisions of the work are on *lakshana*, *pratyaksha*, and *anumāna* (fol. 31 *a*). In the chapter which appears (for the MS. is unfortunately incomplete) to be the last, we find an inquiry into the authority of the *āgamas* which form to the Jain philosopher *çabda* or the 'Word.' The text is written in a fine bold hand and is accompanied by brief marginal glosses containing references to Jain literature, *e.g.* the Vītarāgakathā (f. 31 *a*), and to Buddhist teaching (ff. 28 *b*, 31 *a*).

Lumpāka-mata-kuṭṭana.

Lumpāka-mata-kuṭṭana is the subscription of a short work (of 21 leaves). Outside is written in a much later hand 'Lokāyata-kuṭṭana.' The Lumpāka mata was a school founded in Vikr. Saṃvat 1508 (A.D. 1461). See Dr Klatt in *Ind. Antiq.* XI. 256 (September 1882). The treatise is in the main a compilation from the Siddhānta or canon of the Çvetāmbaras and begins: नत्वा श्रुतज्ञानमनंतभेदं। पारंगतं चेतसि सन्निधाय। सिद्धान्त-वाक्यानि करोमि सम्यक्। Its compilers belonged to the Kharatara-gaccha and wrote the work in Saṃvat 1687.

Upadeça-rasāla.

Another work of similar dimensions and date is the *Upadeçarasāla* by Sādhuraṅga pupil of Bhuvanasoma, (also of the Kharatara-gaccha) composed in V. S. 1587 (A.D. 1530). The MS. was written in Saṃvat 1656 (A.D. 1599), during Jinacandra's pontificate. The subject is ethical, and the language Sanskrit with Prakrit citations.

Vicāra-saṅgraha.

On various subjects connected with religious ordinances and discipline we have a *Vicāra-saṅgraha* or *Paramita-vicārā-mṛita saṅgraha*, being a collection of 25 *vicāras* (examinations?).

The title of the first is *Jinapravacana-svarūpa-vicāra.* The last relates to the ground-whisks and 'respirators' (मुखवस्त्रिकारजोहरण) to prevent the destruction of insect life, which I saw myself in actual use among Jain monks. The work is in Sanskrit, with numerous citations from the canonical, and other Prakrit, books.

Another work not previously noticed, I think, is the *Vicārasāraprakaraṇa* or *Mārgaṇaçataka*, of 117 Prakrit verses, with a very full Sanskrit commentary, terminating with a paṭṭāvalī of the Kharatara-gaccha.

I also collected, wherever I could, *Paṭṭāvalīs* (lists of Jain pontiffs and teachers). The publication of several such lists by Dr Klatt in the *Indian Antiquary* for 1882 has proved most useful. I hope to publish those that I have collected, and trust that we may in time thus get material for a regular table of Jain chronology, which cannot fail to be of the greatest use for general Indian history.

Guṇa-varma-caritra by Maṇikya-sundara Sūri.

In the extensive literature of Jain folk-lore a new acquisition is the *Guṇavarmacaritra*, a work in Sanskrit verse by Maṇikya-sundara Sūri of the Añcala-gaccha, the author of the Pṛithvī-candacarita, of which a MS. exists in the Berlin library. For purposes of identification, especially as the work has another title in the margin, *Çatarabhedaka*[thā ?], I may mention that the opening of the tale relates how Guṇavarmā son of Naravarmā, king of Hastināpur, and Līlavatī his queen go to the *svayaṃvara* of Guṇāvalī daughter of the king of Campā (Bhagalpur). The moral of the tale is the duty of proper religious observance (*pūjā*).

Vratakathākoça by Çrutisāgara.

Another large collection of tales is the *Vratakathākoça* or *Vratopākhyāna-kathā* composed by Çrutisāgara, *Bhaṭṭāraka-Çrī-Mallibhūshaṇa-bhaṭṭārakagurūpadeçāt.* It consists of 24 stories in numbered Sanskrit verses, related in order to illustrate the merit of observing fasts and holy-days. Numerous parallels to this are to be found in the Buddhist literature of Nepal, as for example the tale in praise of the Ashṭamī-vrata (*Catal.* pp. 15, 73). The first tale of the present series is called Jyeshṭha-jinakathā.

Similar to this collection is a tale in 150 verses of which the colophon runs: *iti çrī-kārttike saubhāgyapañcamīmāhātmya-vishaye Varadatta-Guṇamañjarī-kathānakam.* Varadatta-Guna-mañjarī-kathā.

The *Jaya-tihuyaṇa* (tribhuvana)-*vṛitti* is a Prakrit hymn in 30 verses with a Sanskrit commentary and an introductory tale told in Sanskrit, of the sickness, nocturnal vision, cure and subsequent votive offering of Abhayadeva Sūri at Sthambana(-ka)-pur in Gujarat. Jaya-ti-huyaṇa-vṛitti.

§ 3. NOTES ON MSS. IN PRIVATE POSSESSION, NOT ACQUIRED, OF WHICH COPIES COULD BE MADE FOR THE LIBRARY.

Besides the MSS. in the great libraries of Kathmandu and Jeypore, and those in the Government College Library at Benares, of which some account has been given in Part I., I noted a number of MSS. of which copies could be made for the Library, or actually had been made. Indeed it was my constant endeavour to induce owners of books to show me all the good MSS. they possessed, whether they were willing to part with them in every case or not.

In Nepal I was offered a copy of the *Bhadrakalpāvadāna*. As I had not sufficient data to show whether this was not a copy made by the owner previous to the sale of an original to Dr D. Wright (Add. 1411, Catalogue, p. 88), I declined to purchase it. But I am not sure whether the MS. might not be worth purchasing, even with this risk, owing to its rarity and interest.

At Benares I examined the following MSS., of which the owner would willingly send copies, made at the rate of 2 to 3 rupees (3 to 5 shillings) per thousand *çlokas* (of 32 syllables). As a specimen of the style of writing to be expected from Benares scribes, the wellwritten MS. of the Khaṇḍanoddhāra-ṭīkā in my collection (see under *Darçana*, p. 44), obtained from the same Pandit, may be noted. The MSS. in question are chiefly old copies of philosophical works. Following the example of Dr F. Hall in his Bibliographical Index, I mention the date in every case where I observed it, as it may be of value in fixing the age of the commentary-literature, much of which is of course of recent, and indeed contemporary, origin.

(1) A commentary by Çaṅkara Miçra on the Khaṇḍana-khaṇḍa-khādya, a work which, like the Sarvadarçanasaṅgraha, reviews the different schools of Indian philosophy. Commentaries on this work appear to be very rare. The only mention I can find of it is in the Index of Hall, who had heard of it but had not seen it.

The remaining works are chiefly of the Nyāya and Vaiçeshika schools.

(2) Nyāyavārttika. A portion of this work will shortly be printed by Pandit Vindhyeçvarīprasād at Benares. A copy of this MS. is ready.

(3) Part of Vācaspati Miçra's Nyāyavārttika-tātparya, the Pramāṇa-lakshaṇa, about a quarter of the whole. Dated Lakshmaṇa Saṃvat 417 (A.D. 1523).

(4) Nyāyakandalī. Copied from a MS. dated Saṃv. 54 of Kashmir. This work appears to be unknown.

(5) Guṇaprakāçavivṛiti by Bhagīratha. Dated (in words) Çaka 1521 (A.D. 1599).

Amongst MSS. in private possession I may mention two that I noted in one of the lists of books in the Bāla Sarasvati Library (see above p. 25) during the very short time I was there, because the MSS. here, as stated above, are not in all cases given to the Library, though copies can be had.

(6) A commentary on the Caraṇavyūha.

(7) A *dīpikā* on the *ṭīkā* of the Hastāmalaka.

APPENDICES.

I. Inscriptions.

II. Rough list of MSS. in the Jain Mandir, Benares.

III. Addenda to my Catalogue of Buddhist MSS., with notices of criticisms.

APPENDIX I.

INSCRIPTIONS.

Table.

I.	At Bhātgāon, Nepal;	dated [Gupta]	Saṃvat	318	(A.D. 637).
II.	At Patan, Nepal;	dated [Çrī-Harsha]	Saṃvat	34	(A.D. 640).
III.	„ „	„	„ „	82	(A.D. 688).
IV.	At Kathmandu, Nepal		„ „	151	(A.D. 757).
V.	At Patan „		[Nepal] Saṃvat	203	(A.D. 1083).
VI.	„ „		„ „	259	(A.D. 1139).
VII.	At Amber, Rajputana;		Saṃvat	1011	
VIII.	At Aṛ, Mewar; (x—xith cent.).				
IX.	Patan, Nepal;		Nepal Saṃvat	512	(A.D. 1392).

It will be seen from the above list that the present series affords a more continuous representation of the progress of writing on stone in Nepal than has hitherto been published, which of course gives an interesting parallel to the palæography of the MSS. in our library already described by me. The phraseology, technical terms etc. correspond closely with the published series. See *Indian Antiquary*, IX. 168 sqq., and XIV. 342.

In some of the earlier inscriptions chronological points of considerable importance will be found.

The transcripts now given are prepared from squeezes made by myself on the spot, and in some cases also from photographs made by me from the stone. I have also received some additional squeezes of a few of the Nepal series from Pandit Indrānand. Much still remains undeciphered which probably a second visit to the places might enable me to determine, and something further, no doubt, might here and there be got out of my present materials. But, as I have said already, the pressure of other work and want of leisure by daylight renders it undesirable to delay publication.

I. Slab of stone, 18 inches wide, at Golmāḍhi-ṭol, Bhātgāon. Dated [Gupta-] saṃvat 316 or 318 (A.D. 635-7).

For further particulars see above p. 13 and add a reference to the article on Nepalese chronology in the *Indian Antiquary* for Dec. 1885 (p. 342), where Mr Fleet notes that this inscription 'supplies the keynote' to the interpretation of the early series. As to the units' figure which at p. 13 I have given as 8 I am somewhat uncertain. The symbol, which seems to me to be a numeral-figure and not an *akshara* or letter-numeral like the others, resembles most nearly the 6 in our most archaic Nepalese MS., Add. 1702 (see the table in my Catalogue), though there also 8 is very similar.

[1] स्वस्ति मानगृहादपरिमितगुणसमुदयोद्भा[सितदि]-
शो व-

[2] प्पपादानुद्ध्यातो लिच्छविकुलकेतुर्भट्टारकमहारा-
जश्रीशिवदे-

[3] वः कुशली माखोष्टंसत्सरद्रङ्गनिवासिनः प्रधान-
[जनपुर]स्सरा-

[4] न्ग्रामकुटुम्बिनः कुशलपरिप्रश्नपूर्व्वं समाज्ञाप[यति]
विदि-

[5] तम्भवतु भवतां यथानेन प्रख्या[तामल]विपुल – –
– – प-

[6] राक्रमोपशमितामितविपक्षप्रभावेन महासामन्तां-
शुवर्म्म-

[7] णा विज्ञापितेन मयैतद्गौरवाद्युष्मदनुकम्पया च कूबेर्व्व-

VIII.

INSCRIPTION NO. 1.

Photographed by the Author.

[8] त्यधिकृतानामत्र समुचितस्त्रिकरमात्रसाधनायैव प्रवे-

[9] शो लेख्यदानपञ्चापराधाद्यर्थन्त्वप्रवेश[1] इति प्र-
सादो वः

[10] कृतस्तदेवंवेदिभिरस्मत्प्रसादोपजीविभिरन्यैर्वा न

[11] कैश्चिदयमन्यथाकरणीयो यस्त्वेतामाज्ञां विलङ्घ्या-
न्यथा कु-

[12] र्य्यात्कारयेद्वा तमहमतितरान्न मर्षयिष्यामि ये
वास्मदू-

[13] र्द्ध्वम्भूभुजो भवितारस्तैरपि धर्म्मगुरुभिर्म[- -कृ]-
तप्रसा-

[14] दानुवर्त्तिभिरियमाज्ञा सम्यक्परिपालनीयेति समा-
ज्ञापना

[15] दूतकश्चात्र भोगवर्म्मा स्वामी (*sic*) संवत् ३१६ ज्येष्ठ-
शुक्लदिवा दशम्याम्

Translation.

Hail! From Mānagṛiha. The illustrious Çivadeva, meditating on the feet of Bappa, who has illuminated the quarters by the dayspring of his countless virtues, being in good health, to the cultivators resident in the villages of Mākhoshṭam and Satsaradraṅga (?) under the lead of their headmen, with due enquiries after their health, addresses the following order:—

"Be it known to you that, at the request of the great

[1] *I.e.* apparently, not for purposes of criminal or corrective procedure. This usage of apraveça seems to throw some light on the form and meaning of the Prakrit apāvesa in the inscription in the Pandulena cave No. 3, as to which Pandit Bhagvānlāl in his learned article in the Bombay Gazetteer (s.v. Nasik) expresses doubt.

feudatory Aṃçuvarman, who by his renowned...doughty and ...prowess has subdued the might of his innumerable foes, out of regard for him and compassion for you, I grant you this boon, namely that the officials of Kūbervatī[1] are allowed entrance for the levying only of not more than the three taxes, but not for granting writings or for the five offences and the like[2]. Therefore this boon must not be infringed by our dependants who have cognisance of this, nor by any other parties whatsoever: and whosoever, in contravention of this order, does so infringe or cause infringement, him I will in no wise suffer; moreover such kings as shall be after us, ought, as guardians of religion and (*thus*) as followers of grants (*made...*), to preserve my order in its entirety. In this matter the executive officer is Bhogavarman Svāmin. Saṃvat 316, on the 10th of the bright fortnight of Jyeshṭha."

II. Slab of stone, 14 inches wide, in a place called Sundhārā[3], Patan, Nepal; dated [Çrī-Harsha] Saṃvat 34 (A.D. 640). See pp. 7–8 above.

Doubtful readings are indicated by dots placed under the letters.

1. — कैला[स]कूटभवनाद्भगवत्पशुपति
2. बप्पपादानुध्यातः श्री म[हा]सा[मन्तांशुवर्म्मा]
3. -- वर्तमानभविष्यतो
4. समाज्ञपयति विदित[मस्तु] भवताम — —
5. — — नृपकुलमथ विनिपतितेष्टकापङ्क्तिविवरप्रविष्ट

[1] Qu. 'treasury-officers,' in spite of the somewhat barbarized form.

[2] The five great offences generally enumerated by writers on law and called by them *mahāpātakas* are: (1) murder of a Brahman, (2) theft, (3) adultery with a *guru's* wife, (4) drinking spirituous liquors, (5) intercourse with such as commit these offences. See Manu xi. 55, Vishṇu xxxv. 1—2, Yajñavalkya iii. 227. Dr D. Wright, on the authority (as he informs me) of Pandit Guṇānand only, gives a different list at p. 189 of his History.

[3] This must be the stone referred to by Dr D. Wright in his History p. 246, note. Yet I should hardly call the inscription 'effaced,' though the part above the present level of the street is much worn.

IX.

INSCRIPTION NO. II.

Photographed by the Author

6. नकुलकुलाकुलितमूषिक – – पुर विघटित निरव

7. शेषद्वारकवाटवातायनादिजीर्णदारुसंघातं यत्नतः

8. प्रतिसंस्कार्य तस्य दीर्घतरपश्चात्कालसौस्थित्यनिमित्त

9. [म]क्षयनीविप्रतिबद्धमेवं माटिङ्ग्रामस्य दक्षिणतो राज-

10. भोग्यतामापन्नं विंशतिकय – – षष्टिमानिकपिण्डकां[1] क्षे

11. त्रम् दक्षिणपश्चिमतश्च षण्मानिकापिण्डकम्माटिङ् ग्रामपा

12. ञ्चालिकेभ्यः प्रतिपादितमेवंवेदिभिर्न कैश्चिदस्मत्पाद

13. प्रतिबद्धजीवनैरन्यैर्वायन्न मे धिकारी न्यथा करणीय [:।]

14. यस्त्वेतामाज्ञामुल्लङ्घ्यान्यथा कुर्यात्कारयेद्वा तं वयन्न मा[र्ष]

15. यिष्यामो भवष्यद्भिरपि भूपतिभिर्धर्मगुरुभिर्धर्माधि

16. कारप्रतिपालनादृतैर्भवितव्यम् संवत् ३४ प्रथमपौष

17. शुक्लद्वितीयायाम् [दू]तकोत्र महाबलाध्यक्षविन्दुस्वामी॥

Translation.

From the palace of Kailāsakūṭa [the sovereign[2]] who meditates on the feet of Bappa addresses the following order to the present and future [officials of certain places]: "Be it known to you that...the royal family: now that I have diligently had replaced the mass of decayed wood belonging to the doors, panels, windows etc., which have been entirely destroyed, since the crevices in the layers of bricks that have fallen away have been entered by tribes of ichneumons who

[1] Read पिण्डकं

[2] The name of the great feudatory Aṃçuvarman may be restored with tolerable certainty. Compare the last inscription and number 6 in Pandit Bhagvānlāl's series dating from the same year.

worried the mice [already there], to ensure its good condition for the longer time to come, there has been thus attached as an endowment a field to the south of the village of Mātiṅ, heretofore included in the crown-estate, measuring 20 [measures and producing] the revenue of 60 *mās*; and to the south-west one producing the revenue of 6 *mās* is handed over to the Pāñcālikas of the village of Mātiṅ. My authority herein must not be infringed [etc., as in other inscriptions of Aṃçuvarman]. Saṃvat 34, on the second day of the light half of the first (intercalary) Pausha. My appointed agent herein is Vindusvāmin, chief Minister of War."

The most important point in this inscription is the intercalation occurring in the date. My surmise that an intercalation was referred to in the expression *prathama* was first confirmed by Mr Fleet, to whom I showed my reading, but Professor Bühler of Vienna, to whom I am indebted for much help in deciphering this and the following inscription, called my attention to its great importance. Dr Bühler also kindly submitted the date to the examination of Dr Schram, Privatdocent für chronologische Astronomie at the Vienna University, from whom I have received through Dr Bühler some very elaborate and valuable calculations. I think it would be beyond the scope of the present publication to reproduce these here, but my obligation is none the less. Professor Adams has also most kindly worked out the calculations. From these two eminent authorities I have obtained the following results: (1) that the Nepalese at the time of the inscription used as the basis of their calendar not the Sūrya-siddhānta (in which Pausha is never intercalary, it would seem), but a work that had the same elements as the Brahma-siddhānta; (2) that the year 640 A.D. according to this rule is intercalary, which adds another confirmation, if any be needed, to the theory that the era of this group of inscriptions is that of Çrī-Harsha (A.D. 606).

III. Slab of stone, 15 inches wide, at Gairi-dhārā, Patan, Nepal. Dated [Çrī-Harsha] Saṃvat 82 (A.D. 688).

1. [स्व][स्ति]कैलासकूट[भ]वना[द]

2.

3.

4.

5.

6.

7. तप

8. ले भगवद्वज्रेश्वर प्रण

9. ------ सर्वाधिकरणा ना मप्रविधातव्य नुप्र

10. ------ गण प्रसादीकृतमनेनास्य -- न्तु

11. -- नात्मनः श्रेयोभिवृद्धये धार्मिकगणनमतिसृष्टम्

12. प्रतिपालन प्रतिज्ञा न यो ग कर्म यो गुर

13. ि--- कालमनतिक्रम्य प्रधानम्

14. --- गन्धपुष्पधूपप्रदीपवर्षवर्धनवर्षाकाल

15. -- मन्त्रजपकादिप्रकरणपूजा कर्तव्या पाञ्चाल्याञ्च

16. उपलेपनसम्मार्जनप्रतिसंस्कारादिकं कृत्वा यद्यस्ति

17. परिशेषन्तेन द्रव्येण भगवन्तं वज्रेश्वरमुद्दिश्य

18. पाशुपतानाम्ब्राह्मणानाञ्च यथासम्भवम्भोजनङ्कर

19. णीयन्तदन्यच्च कालान्तरेण यदि कदाचिद्दानपति

20. त्वेन प्रार्थयन्त आपत्सु तत्कालम्बुध्वा दानपतीनाम्

21. धान्यानाश्चतुर्विंशतिर्मानिका देया अतो धिकन्[द]ानप

22. तिभिर्न ग्राह्यं यदा चात्र कार्यमुत्पद्यते परमासन

23. [म]धिकारमात्तङ्करणीयन्न तु द्रव्यस्याक्षेपस्तदेव

24. [म]वगत सर्वाधिकरणाधिकृतैरन्यैर्वा न कश्चिदयम्[1]

25. अस्मत्प्रसादो न्यथा कर्त्तव्यो ये त्वस्मदाज्ञां व्यतिक्रम्य वर्त[न्ते]

26. वयन्तेषान्न मर्षयामो ये प्यस्मदूर्ध्वम्भवितारो राजा

27. नस्तैरपि पर्वनृपतिकृतप्रसादप्रतिपालनाद्द

28. तैर्नान्यथा करणीयं स्वयमाज्ञा दूतकश्चात्र भट्टार

29. [क]युवराज स्कन्ददेवः संवत् ८२ [भाद्र] पद शुक्ल दि

30. — — म् ॥ ॥

Translation.

From the palace of Kailāsakūṭa................................ (ll. 11, 12) for [his] own increase of prosperity the enumeration of the righteous[2]...handed over [for] protection[2]...(l. 13) not overstepping the due time, worship must be performed having as its occasion [the offering of] spells charms etc. for [hastening] the rainy season and for increasing rain[3] and odours, flowers, incense, lights...; and with the Pāñcālī-community, after having done all such business as smearing with cow-dung, cleansing and repairs, if a residue remains, with that money in honour of the blessed Vajreçvara[4] a feast is to be made, as far as means

[1] Read कैश्चिद°

[2] These phrases cannot be translated with any certainty without more context. *Dhārmikagaṇanam* is perhaps to be compared with *Guṇigaṇagaṇana* in Pañcatantra, Introd. 8. (=Hitop. Introd. 15). *Atisṛishṭam pratipālanāya* occurs in Bhagvānlāl's Inscr. No. 7, line 14.

[3] A specimen of this class of *pūjā* is the *Megha-sūtra*, edited by me in the R. A. S. Journal for 1880.

[4] 'To gain [a god's] favour', B. and R. s. v. ud-diç. *Vajreçvarī* and

X.

INSCRIPTION NO. III.

A photographic reproduction of part of the back of a paper squeeze

XI.

1. INSCRIPTION REFERRED TO AT PAGE 14, LINE 8.

2. " NO. IV. SEE PAGES 4, 79.

3. " NO. VII. " 29, 81.

From squeezes.

allow, to the Pāçupata ascetics and Brahmans; and in case perchance on another occasion, on the strength of their being benefactors, people ask for something else than this, in times of need, then, after you have ascertained that this is the proper time for it, 24 *mānikās* of grain may be given to benefactors; more than this is not to be taken by the benefactors. Now when a law-suit arises[1] as to these points, the Supreme Court is to be constituted the standard (?) of authority[2]; but the money must not be thrown away. With this understanding neither the fully authorised officer nor any other parties whatsoever may controvert this boon, (etc., as in the other inscriptions).

Our appointed agent in this matter is the heir apparent Skandadeva[3]. Saṃvat 82, Bhādrapada, bright half…

IV. Water-conduit slab near the temple of Jaisi, Kathmandu. Dated [Çrī-Harsha] Saṃvat 151 (A.D. 757). See p. 4, above.

1. ७ संवत् १५१ वैशाख शुक्ल द्वितीयायाम्
2. लञ्जग्वल्याञ्चाकाय[ा]न्नित्योपभोगार्थम्
3. अतीतलम्भस्य भार्याया[4] भोजमत्या दत्तम्
   …   …
4. जलद्रोणेन सह — — मा २ ॥ ॥

Vajrapāṇi are Buddhist divinities; and as the *vajra* is very rarely Sivaic, while Vaishnavism is very little known in Nepal, it seems fair to infer that we find here early traces of the curious juxtaposition of Hindu and Buddhist cult that the Tantric system brought into Nepal.

1 Cf. Manu 8. 43.

2 The exact force of *mātra* is not easy to express. It cannot well have its common meaning 'merely'; if it does not convey anything of its radical meaning of measure, as suggested above, it probably serves only to give slight additional definition or emphasis to *adhikāra*.

3 I could not discern any remains of the *k* on the stone but *s* (conjunct) and *nd* were fairly distinct; and, though not clear in the squeeze from which the autotype has been prepared, in another squeeze made by me the *n* conjunct comes out very well and the *s* and *d* very fairly. Observe that the *d* is written *below* in the conjunct न्द in Gupta writing. The (*akshara*) form of 80 is also much clearer in this squeeze. I am not sure whether the unit-figure is 2 or 3.

4 Read भार्यया.

"Saṃvat 151, on the second day of the light half of Vaiçākha, Bhojamati wife of Atītalambha gave two mās [of land ?] to the Pañch-committee of Lañjagval, together with a water-receptacle, for their perpetual enjoyment thereof."

What *jaladroṇa* may mean precisely I have no means of telling; and the dictionaries give no help. I at first thought from the position of the stone and from a possible connexion with √dru 'run' that it must mean water-*course*, like *praṇāli*: but the ordinary meaning of *droṇa*, 'tub', rather suggests a reservoir; and to this view Dr Bühler, I find, is inclined. The word *droṇa* occurs also in the next inscription, and there the first meaning is perhaps more probable. The gradual approximation to Kuṭila forms in the characters of this inscription is noticeable, particularly in the lengthened and more sweeping *curves* of medial *ā* and *ī*.

V. Dedicatory verses on the pedestal of a figure of the sun-god, Patan, Nepal. Dated [Nepal] Samvat 203 (A.D. 1083).

See pp. 8–9 with plate. Space covered by inscription, $5\frac{1}{2} \times 2\frac{3}{4}$ inches.

1. ७ त्रिभिर्वर्षैः समायुक्ते संवत्सरशतद्वये । वैशाखशु
2. क्लशप्तम्यां [*sic*] बुधे पुष्योदये शुभा [॥] श्रीयशोदेवभूनाथत
3. नयो धर्मतत्परः । श्रीवाणदेवः कृतवान् प्रतिमां सु
4. प्रतिष्ठिता[ं] । दिवाकरस्य या मात्रा पुरा संकल्पिता मुदा
5. कर्तुस्तेनास्तु सततं तेजोवृद्धिरनुत्तरा ॥ ० ॥

Translation.

When two hundred years were joined with three, on the 7th of the bright half of Vaiçākha, on Wednesday, Pushyā was auspicious at its rising. Vāṇadeva son of king Yaçodeva, religiously disposed, made [this] image well set up in honour of the Sun, which had previously been planned by his mother with

XII.

INSCRIPTION NO. VI.

From a squeeze.

rejoicing. Therefore to the maker may there ever accrue supreme increase of glory!

It is interesting to compare the forms of the letters of Add. 1684 in our library (*Catal.* pp. xxv. 173 and Table of Letters) with those of this inscription.

VI. Inscription of Mānadeva's reign, dated Nepal Saṃvat 259 (A.D. 1139). See p. 10 above.

१ सम्वत् २५९ भाद्रपद कृष्ण सप्तम्यां । श्रीमत् राजाधिराज परमेश्वर (2) परमभट्टारक । श्रीमानदेवस्य वि-जयराज्ये । श्री दनीश्व[र]दक्षिण धिवा (3) सिन । दिवंशत-पजनवननिर्म्मितेन तत्रैव । यो धिवासिन । द्रोनमेव (4) नद्या: तत पन्नालि कर्त्तव्यम् नित्यवच्छिन्नन् सम्प्रदत्तं

This inscription is reproduced only on account of its date and style of writing. One might well suppose it to have been scratched on the stone by a second-rate MS. copyist, for both the incision and the attempt at Sanskrit are unusually feeble for an inscription of such a date; so much so that I have not attempted a translation. It records the gift of a water-channel (*pannāli* of course for *praṇāli*) and a *droṇa* (see last inscription).

The great interest of the discovery is that we find here an instance, unique as far as I know, of the use of the peculiar local *hooked hand* of Nepal which has been abundantly illustrated in the Palæographical Society's Oriental Series as well as in my Catalogue.

This and the preceding inscription thus form a link, in point of character, between the periods illustrated by Nos. 1—15 and that of Nos. 16, 17, etc. in Pandit Bhagvānlāl's series.

VII. Tablet in the wall of a temple on a hill above Amber, Rajputana. Date Saṃvat 1011 = A.D. 954, if, as supposed at p. 29 above, the Vikrama era be used.

संवत १०११ भाद्रपदे ब	–भु–द
दि ११ सुक्र दिन ज––तन	रीसुतः
	अददात्

VIII. Fragment built into a staircase at Aṛ, near Oodeypore (Mewar). Width of inscription 3 feet 6 inches. See p. 32.

1. –न्नटी चपटलाधिपतिः समेतः कारंडिकैः सदसि शक्तिकुमारमेव । विज्ञप्तवान्सकलधर्म्मविधानविज्ञः प्रज्ञाप्रकर्ष-चतुरो नृपतिं वचोभिः ॥ द्रम्मानष्ट लभामहे क्षितिप यान्षट्-चक्रमा च्छ्रीमदाघाटम

2. –युक्तकरण्ड–भ–के ब्दं प्रति । ते स्माभिश्चतुर्दशापि तपनायास्मै प्रदत्ता इति श्रुत्वा तेन महीभृता स्ववचनैनैते स्वदत्ताः कृताः ॥ शरीरं जीवितं लक्ष्मीः सर्वं ज्ञात्वेत्यशाश्वतं । भानवे मी प्रदातव्या द्रम्मा भाविनि ये

Translation.

—nnaṭa, the record-keeper[1], attended by the casket bearers (?)[2], in conclave reported to the King, even Çaktikumāra (discerning was he in the ordering of every law and skilled in the pre-eminence of prudence) in these words: "Let us take eight drachms, my liege, which up to the six-fold circle......[offer in] suitable caskets year by year. These fourteen, however, we have offered to yonder sun." When the King heard this he made a free gift of these...by his own word, saying: "We know that body, life, our fortune, all are an unconstant thing: so these drachms are to be offered to the Sun, O lady..."

1 For *akshapaṭalādhipati* compare the inscriptions in the *Indian Antiquary* for 1877, pp. 196, 200.

2 This is a mere guess, for *kāraṇḍika* is not to be found in dictionaries.

XIII.

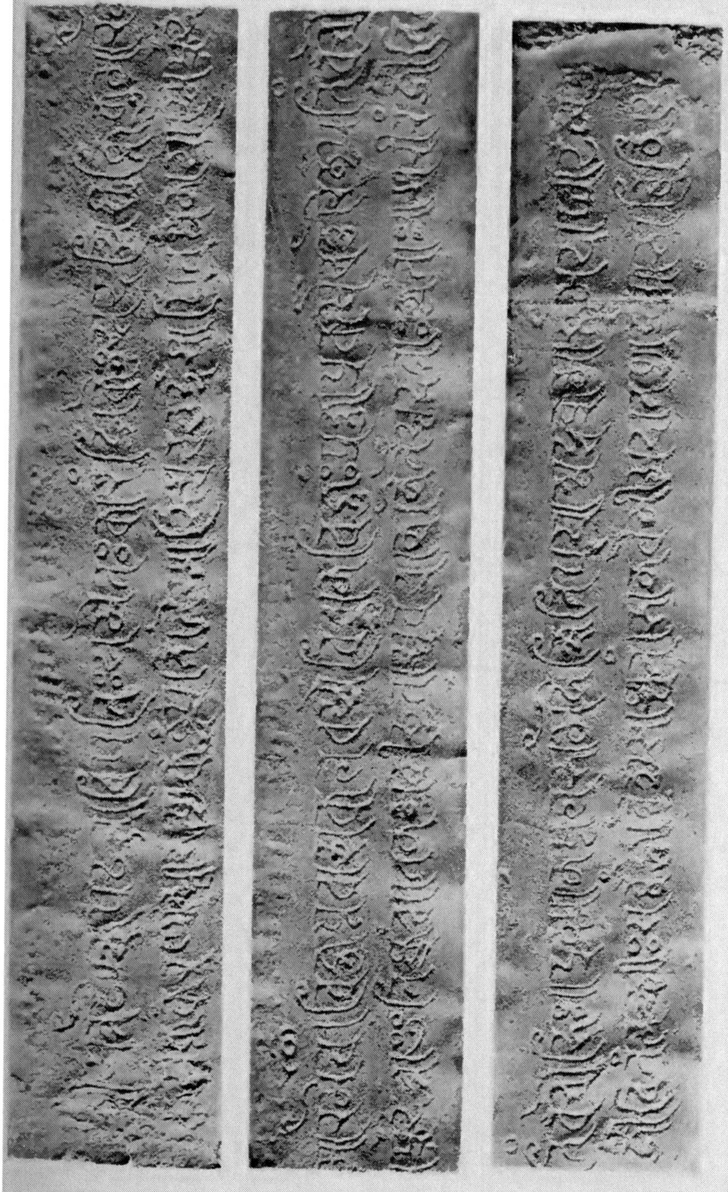

INSCRIPTION NO. VIII.

From a squeeze.

IX. Slab of slate in the courtyard of the temple of Kumbheçvara, Patan, Nepal; dated Nepal Saṃvat 512 (A.D. 1392).

Size of inscribed portion of slab, 1 ft. $4\frac{1}{2}$ in. × 1 ft. $3\frac{1}{2}$ in. Facsimile photographed from my heelball rubbing; see p. 12.

1. स्वस्ति श्रीमन्नेपलिक सम्वत् ५१२ वैशाखकृष्णषष्ठ्यां तिथौ ॥ शरकरणे[1] । विस्तमुहूर्त्ते
2. श्रवणनक्षत्रे । ऐन्द्रयोगे । आदित्य वासरे ॥ श्रीललितपत्तननगरोत्तमे ॥ श्रीश्रीम[न्म]
3. [हा]कुमारसप्तफणावलीमणिकिरणसंद्योतायमान श्रीनागराजाधिष्ठिते ॥ परमेश्वरपरम
4. भट्टारक श्रीमानेश्वरीवरलब्धप्रसाद असुरनारायणेत्यादि विविधविरुदराजावलीपूर्व्व-
5. – – – – क्रियासमालंकृत महाराजाधिराज श्रीश्रीमत् जयस्थिति राज मल्लदेवेन संभुज्यमान
6. [राज्ये] ॥ ॥ श्रीमत्सप्तकुटुम्बजप्रधानमूर्त्थंग महायात्र श्रीचिभयात्रप्रमुखादिभिः संयात्व
7. – ने । श्रीमानीगलोत्तरस्थाने । अस्ति तत्र महातीर्थः कुंभतीर्थ इति स्मृतः । यत्रैष भग-
वान्देवः श्री-
8. [कुं]भेश्वरशंकरः । तस्याग्नेयदिशि स्थाने विघ्नराजस्य वासुकी । दक्षिणे मातरः सर्वाः पितृतीर्थस्य

[1] This must be the Hindustani سركرني.

9. [दुत्त]रे । वायव्या चैव दिग्भागे गौरी पुष्करिणी च ते । ऐशान्यां केशवश्चैवं मध्ये कुंभेश्वरः

10. शिवः ॥ कुंभर्षिमुनिमुख्येन पत्नी – पि तपः कृतं । आराधितो महादेवस्तेन कुंभे-

11. श्वरः स्मृतः ॥ पुष्करिण्या च यत्तोये यः करोत्यवगाहनं । श्रावणे पूर्णिमाश्यां वै सो पि स्वर्ग-

12. [मवा]प्नुयात् ॥ यत्पादाम्बुजसंपूतं निर्म्मलदूरितापदं । प्रणालिकमुखद्वारात्तोयं वहति

13. [नित्]यशः । यत्तीर्थोद्भववारिणा सुनियतं स्नात्वा नरो नित्यशः पीत्वा वारि सुनिर्म्मितं किमथवा कृत्वा

14. मुखक्षालनं । नित्यं यो प्यभिवन्दते प्रतिदिनं श्रीदेवकुम्भेश्वरं भुक्त्वा सर्वसुखानि याति नगरीं सौं-

15. ते पुरां शाम्भवीं बभूव तत्र कुम्भेशः प्रासादरहितः परं । आवासमात्रसंच्छन्न स्थितः कुम्भेश्वरः

16. शिवः । अस्ति पुण्याद्धि संभूतो जयभीमो नरोत्तमः । पार्क्किंसिंको गृहस्थाने समावासी धनेश्वरः

17. ॥ परोपकरव्यवशायशीलो दाता गुणज्ञो हि विवेकी । पुत्रोत्तमो यं गुणवर्म्मणो ऽसौ साक्षा

18. त् हरिश्चन्द्र इवैष धीरः । तस्यांगना महाशीला अनन्तलक्ष्मी विश्रुता । पीडिताज्वरभोगेन मुमू

19. र्च्छ शयने च सा । तां जीवयितुं प्राज्ञोऽसौ जयभीमो विचक्षणः कुंभेश्वरालयं कर्त्तुं प्रतिज्ञा कृ

INSCRIPTION NO. IX.

From a heelball rubbing.

20. तवांस्ततः ॥ न रचिता तथाप्येवं नीता स्वर्गे शिवेन सा । स्वां वाचं प्रतिरक्षार्थं करोति स्म शिवालयं

21. ॥ द्वितीया अभयलक्ष्मी च अभयदेव सुतस्तथा ॥ जयतेजो नुजस्तस्य तेषां सुसंमतेन च ॥ कृत्वा दे

22. वालयं रम्यं प्रासादं हि सतोरणं विशोधीकृत्य भूमिं च प्राकारैः परिवेष्टितं । कृत्वा चातुर्मुखं

23. कोशं सौवर्णं रत्नमण्डितं । ढिःकिणी[1] सुविचित्रां च ढौकित्वा परमेश्वरं । कृत्वा लक्षाहुतिं तस्मिन् वेद

24. घोषैं सुमंगलं । समारोपितवांस्तत्र सुवर्णकलसध्वजं । अनेन कृतपुण्येन चातुर्वर्णोदयो ज

25. नाः । प्राप्नुवंतु महासौख्यमंते च परमम्पदं । येनाकारि महेश्वरस्य भवनं विष्णोस्तथान्यस्य वा तस्मि

26. न् काष्ठशिलेष्टकं निपतितं कुर्व्वंति ये स्थापनं । तेषामेव सुखं भवत्यनुदिनं भूत्वा धनाढ्यं नरास्तेऽ

27. न्ते यान्ति पुरीं शिवस्य नगरीं मोदन्ति तस्मिन्सदा ॥ शुभं भवतु सर्व्वेषां शिवं भवतु सर्व्वदाः ॥ * ॥

[1] Apparently a form of the Hindi ढकनी

Translation (see also abstract at p. 12).

Hail! In the year of Nepal 512, on the 6th lunar day of the dark half of Vaiçākha.

By order of Government. In the Çravaṇa asterism and the Aindra conjunction, Sunday.

In the capital city Lalita-pattana, presided over by the snake-king who is glorious with the rays of the gems of his cluster of seven hoods, the sovereignty being enjoyed by Jayasthiti the sovereign lord, who has gained favour from the bounty of Māneçvarī, whose royal lineage...[is renowned]...in various panegyrics as of the Asuras and Nārāyaṇa, who is adorned by [?mighty] deeds. In the northern region of Mānīgala[1], there is the great *tirth* called Kumbhatīrtha, where lives this venerable God Kumbheçvara[2]. On the south-east side are Gaṇeça and Vāçukī, on the south all the divine Mothers, the *tirth* of the Fathers is to the north, in the north-west quarter are Gaurī and Pushkariṇī in the north-east likewise Vishṇu, and in the centre Kumbheçvara. With Agastya the sage born in the *kumbha* (pitcher) at the head...penance is done: by him Mahādeva is worshipped, and hence called Kumbheçvara, and with the water of the lake whoso makes ablution at the full moon of Çrāvaṇa, even he can obtain heaven.

Cleansed by the lotus of his feet and void of spot, stain or evil, from the mouthpiece of a conduit the water flows perpetually.

With the water from this *tīrth* if a man has strictly washed, and regularly drunk the water well meted out and has performed the rinsing of the mouth, or whoso daily and constantly salutes Kumbheçvara, he enjoys all pleasures and goes at last to the city and town of Çiva. At that place was Çiva destitute of a temple thereupon: Çiva Kumbheçvara abode

[1] I omit the previous sentence as being partly obliterated and partly containing names and allusions, probably local, of which I have no knowledge.

[2] As to this form of Çiva we may compare the Ashṭamīvrata-vidhāna translated by Wilson (Essays, ed. Rost, ii. 32), from which it will be seen that the cult referred to here is of the Tantric school.

under the mere shelter of a dwelling-house. [For the contents of lines 16—23 see p. 12].

(Line 23.) He has also made a variegated cover [for the treasury or treasure-case] approaching the mighty Lord, making thereon an offering of a lac auspicious with sounds of [recitations from ?] the Veda: there too he has erected a golden pinnacle and banner. Through him, the doer of such a good work, may the people sprung from the four castes[1] attain great bliss and a mansion in the highest at the last! The man who makes a dwelling for Çiva and also Vishṇu or some other deity, to him is allotted wood, stone and brick. Such men as set up [the image of a god], to them accrues blessing, day by day becoming riches: those men go to Çiva's city and delight in it for ever.

[1] Read °*odayā* and understand of the Hindus proper as opposed to Buddhists and aborigines.

APPENDIX II.

ROUGH LIST OF MSS. IN THE LIBRARY OF THE JAIN MANDIR AT RĀMGHĀṬ, BENARES.

The following list is transcribed into Roman characters from a copy kindly made for my use, as mentioned at p. 24 above. I give it in the form I received it, only correcting a few obvious mistakes and not attempting to reconstruct the names of the less known works. It will be noted that the collection includes several of the Brahmanical works, (such as the poems of Kālidāsa) often found in Jain libraries, as well as numerous tracts in the vernaculars, as to which I have little knowledge.

No. of library case.		No. of leaves.
1.	Bhagavatī-vṛitti	626
	Bhagavatī-sūtra	324
3.	Uttarādhyayana	360
	Dīpotsava-vyākhyāna	20
	Uvavāi-ṭabbā	99
	Jñātādharma-vṛitti	74
	Pariçishṭa-parvan	111
	Sūyagaḍānga	45
	Pañca-saṅgraha	39
	Saṃyaktvakaumudī	35
4.	Ṭhānāṅga	78
	Chaitri-pūnima-vyākhyāna (?)	3
	Jñātā [dharma]-sūtra-ṭabba	317
	Nirayāvalī-sūtra-ṭabba	73
	Upāsakadaçā	57
	Rāyapaseṇipañcapāta(?)	110

No. of library-case.		No. of leaves.
	Sādhupratikramaṇa-bālabodha	10
	Guṇasthānakramaroha-mūla	15
5.	Hemī Nāmamālā	102
	Ācārāṅga	96
	Paṇṇāvaṇā	340
	Kumārasambhava-kāvya	20
	Antagaḍadaçā	11
	Nirayāvalī	39
	Upadeçamālā	
	Gajasiṃha-carita	125
	Çilopadeçamālā	104
6.	Kalpadrumakulika	182
	Ashṭābdhi-kāvyākhyāna	12
	Kalpasūtra	75
	Daçamīkalikā (? vaikāl°)	38
	Tarkabhāshā	23

No. of library-case.		No. of leaves.
	Tarkasaṅgrahasamagra	1
	Kalpa-kir[a]ṇāvalī	229
	Bhartṛihari-prathama-dvitīyaçataka-ṭīka	37
	Bhartṛihari-tritīya	17
	Dharmapāṭha	62
7.	Çrīpalacopāī [Hindi]	29
	Vipākasūtra	74
	Prathamakrama-grantha sūtra	25
	Çrāddha-vidhi	42
	Saṅgrahaṇī-vṛitti	98
	Uttarādhyayana	267
8.	Uvasaggahara-ṭīkā	9
	Ashṭādhyāyī	38
	Aniṭ-akārikā-tripāṭa	6
	Sārasvata (uttarārddha)	42
	Amaradattamitrananda rāsa	40
	Vasūpūjyasvāmi-rāsa	22
	Nala-Davadantī-copāī	38
	Kaya-valhā (?) copāī	18
	Copolī-copāī	11
	Rātribhojana-copāī	15
	Caṃdarāsa	72
	Gāthāsahasrī	40
	Kālagrahaṇāvidhī	15
	Vicāra-çataka	38
	Varshatantra-ṭīkā	36
	Nāracandra prathama prakaraṇa	19
	Dvādaçabhāvaphalam	9
	J[y]otisha-ṭīkā	8
	Sindūraprakaraṇa	30
	Dānaçīla-codhāliyo	9
9.	Pañcakarma-grantha-yantra	56
	Gautama-pṛicchā	53
	Meru-trayodaçī-vyākhyāna	11
	Munipati-caritra gadya	52
	Nigoda-chabīçī-saṭīkā	7
	Caüsaraṇa-paiṇṇā-ṭabbā	7
	Nīlakaṇṭha-tājikā	26
	Sārasvata	63
10.	Rasacandrikā	24
	Vāgbhaṭa-alaṅkāra	8
	Sūryaprajñapti	98
	Dṛishṭāntaçataka-ṭabbā	19
	Vaiyākaraṇa-bhūshaṇa	35
	Sandehaviçodhi	51
	Sadbhāshitāvalī	14
	Haima-çabdānuçāsana	11
	Samarasāra-ṭīkā	14
	Sāmudraka	13
	Comm. on part of Madhava's Nidāna	11
	Vaidyavinoda	18
	Sūtra çṛiṅgāra (?)	5
	Bālavicāra (?) dharma ke phuṭhakaro (?)	20
11.	Shaḍdarçanasamuccaya-ṭīkā	75
	Candapaññatti-ṭīkā	199
	Sūyapaññatti-sūtra.	94
	Yogaçāstradīpikā	253
12.	Siddhānta-candrikā	116
	Sārasvata-ṭīkā Mādhavī	117
	Prabodhacandrikā	20
13.	Mahīpālacaritra prākṛita-gāthā vadha (?)	51
	Saṃvapradyuna rāsara-khaṃḍa (??)	17
	Mṛigāvalī rāsa	27
	Karmagrantha 4 bāla-bodha	115

No. of library-case.		No. of leaves.
	Siddhāṃ[ta]kebolvicāra	27
14.	Janmapatra-paddhati	289
	Laghukaumudī	110
	Kalpakaumudī	274
15.	Jambu-adhyeyana-ṭabbā	63
	Çāntinātha-caritra-gadya	230
	Çātruñjayamāhātmya-ṭabbā	282
16.	Raghuvaṃça	110
	Jñānārṇava-padya (?)	124
	Çrīpāla caritra-gadya	33
	Loka... vṛitti (?)	8
	Ātma-prabodha	137
17.	Guṇa-kramārohavṛitti	26
	Antagaḍaçā	27
	Navatattva-vicāra-ṭabbā	10
	Shaḍāvaçyaka-vṛitti	86
	Uttarādhyayana-ṭīkā Nemicandra-kṛitā	166
	Sattarīsaya-gaṇa	29
	Uvavāi-ṭīka	82
18.	Mahādaṇḍaka	30
	Annadāna-vishaye Bhojakathā	49
	Haima-Anekārthasaṅgraha	70
19.	Shaṭ karmagranthāḥ [or 'Shaṭ-sūtra']	8
	Tarkaparibhāshā	18
	Navatattva-bālabodha	158
	Upadeçamālā-vivaraṇa	77
	Kavi-taraṅga vaidyaka	44
	Jīva[vi]cāra-navatattva-vṛitti	45
	Haima-daṇḍaka	27
20.	Paṇṇāvaṇā-vṛitti	336
	Shaḍāvaçyaka-ṭabbā	33
	Nirayāvalī	43
	Kathākoça-gadya	86
21.	Ḍhālasāgara	225
	Pārçvanāthacaritra-gadya	79
	Praçnavyākaraṇa-ṭabbā	202
22.	Haima-lingānuçāsana	140
	Haima-anekārtha	40
	Çabda-ratnākara	26
	Vāṇi-bhūshaṇa	23
	Piṅgala	43
	Rāmavinoda	71
	Saṅghayana-bālabodha	71
	Vaidyajīvana	25
23.	Rāmacaritra-gadya	133
	Madanavinoda-nighaṇṭu	89
	Kautuka-patra	24
	Vasantarāja-racita-çākuna-çāstra	137
	Madanavinoda-nighaṇṭu	107
24.	Çakuntalā-nāṭaka	75
	Sugati paṃkshā (?)	41
	Nīlakaṇṭhajātaka-paddhati	46
	Jyotisha-ratnamālā	49
	Vedāntasāra	18
	Kirātārjunīya-kāvya	108
	Kumārasambhava-kāvya	482
	[Of cases 25—30, 33—4, 36—41 no account.]	
31.	Vipākasūtra-ṭīkā	30
	Ratna kalarāsa (?)	91
	Hari[ç]cand[r]a-nṛipa-copaī	53
	Vimala-rāsa	44
32.	Mantra-mahodadhi	60
	Çārī[ra]ka-bhāshya	160

No. of library-case.		No. of leaves.
35.	Uttarādhyayana-vṛitti	210
	Gacchācāra-paiṇṇā-vṛitti	140
	Paṇṇāvaṇā-vṛitti	249
	Saṃbo[dha]sattari	55
	Caüsaraṇā-payannā-tripāṭha-vṛitti	19
	Praçnavyākaraṇa-ṭabbā	108
42.	Pāṇḍavacaritra	163
43.	Paṇṇāvaṇā-sūtra	108
	Nalacaritra-çloka-baddha (?)	148
	Dutāṅgadā-chāyā-nātaka	12
	Adhyātma-kalpadruma	7
	Alaṃkāra-mañjarī	6
44.	Prabodha-cintāmaṇi	46
	Pravacanasāroddhāra-mūla	24
	Rāyapaseṇi-pañca-sāṭha (?)	110
	Nyāyamañjushā-vṛitti	67
	" -mūla	2
	Saṅgrahaṇī-ṭīkā	41
	Tarkaparibhāshā	13
	Jyotisharatnamālā	25
	Nidānajana	12
	Gāthā-ratna-koça	23
	Caüsaraṇa-bālabodha	12
	Nandī-sūtra	22
45.	Prākṛitavyākaraṇa	96
	Tājikasāravṛitti	79
	Prākṛita-manorama	17
	Çrīpālacaritra-saṭīka	155
46.	Pūjāshṭa-phalavishaye kathā	28
	Çravaṇa-bhūshaṇa	6
	Nandīçvarastava-vṛitti	25
	Rasataraṅgiṇī	17
	Ratnāvalī nāṭikā	28
	Daça dṛishṭāntāḥ	30
	Sphoṭa-candrikā	16
	Jambūdvīpa-paññattī sūtra	108
	Nemicaritra padya	
	Ṛishi-maṇḍala-prakaraṇa saṭīka	
47.	Lokaprakāça citra-sahita	452
	Vicāraratnākara	186
	Baṅga culiyāe sūya-hīluppakkhī (?) ajjha-yaṇa	10
	Mahāniçītha-sūtra	95
	Lalitavistara	44
	Aṅgaculiyā sūtra	
48.	Sūyagaḍaṃga-dīpikā	55
	Jātakalpa sūtra	4
	Ammati-sūtra	8
	Sukṛitasāgara	33
	Hemoṇādigaṇasūtra-vivaraṇa (?)	33
	Praçnottara-sārddhaça-takabhāshā	34
	Syādvāda-mañjarī	
50.	Mānasāgarapaddhati	124
	Jātakatattva	38
	Haimaḍhunḍhi-jainen-dravyākaraṇa Laghu-ṭīkā	132
51.	Pratyekabuddha-copāī	26
	Ācārāṅga-sūtra	59
	Vastupāla-Tejapāla copāī	34
	Samavāyāṅga-sūtra	37
	Siṃghāsanabattīsī	75
	Saṅgrahaṇī-vṛitti	64

APPENDIX III.

Revised Chronological Tables of the kings of Nepal, showing additional dates and particulars gained since the publication of my "Catalogue of Buddhist MSS. ...with notices...of the chronology of Nepal", chiefly during my visit to the country.

General Addenda to that work, with notices of criticisms.

TABLE I.

(Compare Catalogue, pp. xi.—xii. of the Introduction. Additional dates etc. are indicated in full-faced type.)

General Table of the Rājas of Nepal (1008—1457 A.D.), with dates from manuscript and other sources.

Name of King	Dates (A.D.) derived from MSS.	Place and No. of MS.	No. of years in reign acc. to Vamç. and Gorkha histt.	Reign acc. to Kirkpatrick, Prinsep and Hodgs. papers.	Notes
Nirbhaya } Rudra }	1008	Add. 866	not named	7	} On the co-regents at this time see the Catalogue, p. v.
Bhoja } Rudra } Lakshmīkāma }	1015	Add. 1643	8	8	
Lakshmīkāma	1039	Add. 1683	22	22	
Jaya-deva	—	—	20	20	
Udaya	—	—	not named	8 K; not in H	According to Kirkpatrick, Bhāskara was a 'refractory tributary of Pātan'; according to the Vamçāvali, the founder of a new dynasty. Clearly the succession was broken here, some of these kings being contemporary rivals.
Bhāskara	—	—	13 G {yrs not in V.	7 H; not in KP	
'Bāl-deva'	—	—	12 G "	{ 11 P { 12 KH	
Pradyumnakāma-deva	1065	**{ Fragment with new MS.** { Add. 1684	11 G "	7	
Nāgārjuna-deva	—	—	3 G "	3	
Çaṅkara-deva	**1071—2**	**Beng. As. Soc. A. 15**	11 G "	17	**'Saṃvat 191 having elapsed' (प्रयाते).**
[Vāṇa', or] Vāma-deva	**[c. 1083]**	**Inscription**	3 G "	2	**See p. 8 above.**
[Rāma]-Harsha-deva	**1093**	**New MS.**	15 G "	16	**MS. now with Dr Hörnle. See p. 46.**
Sadāçiva-deva	—	—	21 G "	28	
[Indra-deva]	—	—	not named	[12]	
Māna-deva	1139	Add. 1643	10	5	**Compare p. 10.** Reign c. 1130—1140.
Narendra (MS. and KP) = Narasiṃha (VG)	**1141**	**Paris, Burn. 104**	22	7	
Ānanda ('Nanda' VGH)	{ 1165 { 1166	Add. 1693 R.A.S. Lond. 2.	21	20 H; not in KP	Reign c. 1161—82.
Rudra-deva	—	—	7 V 19 G	80*	
Mitra (VG) or Amṛita (KP)	—	—	21	4 KP 30 H	
Arideva	date uncertain	Add. 1648	22	31 H { not named in KP	
[Raṇa-çūra]	1222	Br. M. Or. 2208	not named	not named	
['Sumesar-deva'	—	—	{ not named }	6	
'Raz-kāma'	—	—		no number given	
Anya-malla]	—	—		32	
Abhayamalla	{ **1224** { 1	**MS. 214, Kathmandu library** { Add. 1465 { Brit. M. 2203	{19 G: years not in V.	48	
Jaya-deva	**1257**	**{ MS. in Dr Bhagvanlal's collection**	—	[2]	Jaya is stated to have reigned at Bhatgāon, while Ananta reigned at Kathmandu.
Ananta-malla	{ 1286 { 1302	Brit. M. 1493 Add. 1306	25 V 33 G	34 KP 37 H	Kirkpatrick tells us that in this reign an immigration into Nepal took place in Vikrama Saṃv. 1344 = Nep. Saṃv. 408 (= A.D. 1288).
Kings uncertain for 60 years	—	—	—	—	
Jayārjuna-malla	{ **1364** { 1374 { 1384	**MS. 468, Kathmandu library** Add. { 1689 { 1488	—	—	Not named in any history, genealogy, or inscription.
Jayasthiti-malla	{ 1385 { 1386 { 1389 { 1391 { **1392**	Add. { 1395 { 1698 { 1701 { 1663 **Inscription**	[43]	no years given for reign in KP	{ For this king see the histories and inscr. in Ind. Antiq. for Aug. 1880. As to his reign see Catalogue pp. viii., ix.
[Ratnajyoti(r)-malla]	[1392	Add. 1108]	not named	not named	Not otherwise known: probably a petty chief of the obscure town where the MS. was written.
Joint regency	1400	Add. 1664	—	—	**Compare p. 15 above and** Cat. p. ix.
Regency of Jayadharma-malla	**1403**	**Inscription**			
Jayajyoti(r)-malla	1412	Add. 1649	—	years not given	Not in the Vaṃçāvalī; but see the contemporary inscr. in Ind. Antiq. for Aug. 1880, and cp. Notes 1 and 3.
Yaksha-malla	{ 1429 { 1451 { 1457	Add. { 1703 { 1665 { 1691	43 V 20 G	years not given	After this the division of the kingdom followed.

[*To face page 92.*]

TABLE II.

Revised Table of the Kings of Nepal from the Division of the Kingdom to the Gorkha Conquest.

(Cf. Catalogue, Historical Introduction, p. xvii. Fresh dates now printed in thick type.)

Yaksha-malla (ob. circa A.D. 1460).

Line of Bhatgāon

Dates	King
	Rāya VHD$_6$ (Rāma, G).
	Suvarṇa VG (Bhavana H, Bhuvaṇa D$_6$).
	Prāṇa VGHD$_6$.
	Viçva VGHD$_6$.
A.D. 1572 I. (Volache-ṭol). See p. 14	Trailokya VGHD$_6$.
„ 1628 D$_6$ „ 1633 (Add. 1687) Cf. Add. 1696	Jagajjyotiḥ VGH.
	Narendra V (Nareça H, om. G).
A.D. 1642 (Coin) „ **1667*** Inscr. at temple of Nārāyaṇa	Jagatprakāça VGH.
„ **1663** (Coin)	Jitāmitra VGH.
„ **1695** „ „ **1710** Inscr. at Bhairava temple	Bhūpatīndra VGH.
„ **1722** (Coin) „ **1754** Inscr. (supr. p. 13)	Raṇajita VGH.

Line of Kathmandu

Dates	King
	Ratna VGHI$_{19}$.
	Amara VH [om. GI].
	Sūrya VGHI$_{19}$.
	Narendra VGI$_{19}$ [om. H].
	Mahīndra VGHI$_{19}$.
A.D. 1576 (Add. 1355)	Sadāçiva V, Add. 1355, and Brit. Mus. Or. 2206; om. GHI.
A.D. 1600 Inscr. near Nārāyaṇa temple, Lagan-ṭol, Kathmandu	Çivasiṃha VGHI$_{19}$.
(King of Pātan only, V)	Harihārasiṃha I$_{17}$ & $_{19}$.

Line of Kathmandu

Dates	King
	Lakshmīnarasiṃha
A.D. 1649 I$_{17}$ (cf. I$_{19}$) „ **1654** Inscr. Wright, in pl. 13 „ **1655** Coin, Mh. „ **1656** (Coin) „ 1659 (Add. 1385)	Pratāpa
„ 1669	Cakravartendra or **Jayacakramahendra** (Coin, Mh.) — Cf. V (Wright, p. 220)
„ **1674** Coin, Mh. „ **1679** „ „ **1679** (Coin)	Nṛipendra or **Jayanṛipendra** — Cf. V (Wright, p. 220)
„ **1682** (Coins and Add. 1475) „ **1698** Insor. (v. p. 11 supr.) „ **1701** (Coin)	Bhūpālendra
	Bhāskara

Line of Lalitāpur (Pātan)

Dates	King
A.D. **1631** (Coin) „ 1633 (Add. 1637) „ 1637 (I$_{17}$) „ **1654** (Coin)	Siddhinarasiṃha
„ 1665 (D$_5$) „ **1665** (?) (Coin) „ **1678** Inscr. near Durbar (v. p. 7)	[Çri-]Nivāsa
„ **1686** (Coin) „ **1687** new MSS. „ **1693** „ „ **1700** (Coin) „ **1701** Inscr.**	Yoganarendra or Yogendra
„ 1705	Lokaprakāça (queen dowager, Yogamatī) (I$_{21}$ and Coin)

Coins {1709 Jayavīramahīndra / 1711, 1715 (W. and Mh.) Mahīndrasiṃhadeva}

Dates	King (Kathmandu)	Dates	King (Lalitāpur)
„ **1722** (Coin) „ **1728** (Coin, W.)	Jagajjaya (styled Mahīpatīndra)	„ 1722 (?) (Coin)	Jayayogaprakāça‡
„ **1736** „ „ **1753** „	Jāyaprakāça (later also at Lalitāpur)	„ **1729** „ „ **1731** „	Vishṇu
„ **1749** (Coin, struck apparently in a rebellion; see Wright, p. 224)	[Jyotiḥprakāça]	„ **1742** „ „ **1745** (?) „ W. „ **1753**§	Rājyaprakāça
		No dates from Coins or MSS.	Viçvajit VGH.
		No dates from Coins or MSS.	Dalamardana Sāh VGH.
		No dates from Coins or MSS.	Tejanarasiṃha VGH.

Explanation of Abbreviations. V=Vamçāvali (Dr D. Wright's History of Nepal). G=Gorkha histories, Add. 1160 and B. M. Or. 6. H=Mr Hodgson's papers in the India Office. D=MSS. 5 and 6 in the library of the Deutsche Morgenländische Gesellschaft. I=Inscriptions in the *Indian Antiquary*, Aug. 1880. The coins referred to are in the British Museum, except those marked W, which are in the possession of Professor W. Wright at Cambridge, and those marked Mh., which were kindly lent me by H. E. the late Mahārāja of Nepal, as described at p. 16 above.

NOTES.

* This inscription (see p. 14) has its date expressed by a chronogram (*nagāhimunibhir nepālaçake mite*). Compare Wright's *Nepal*, p. 192. The date on the coin of the reign following is quite clear; so that we have here a discrepancy, which I have no means of explaining.

** In the same courtyard as the inscription of A.D. 1801 mentioned at p. 12.

‡ Yogīndraprakāça, the issuer of a coin dated 742 (A.D. 1722) in the Mahārāja's collection, is apparently the same person.

§ See Dr Rājendralāl Mitra's Introduction to his Lalita Vistara, p. 62, note. He reads the chronogram *agni-muni-nāga* [N. S.] 871; but surely, besides the authority of the regular lists of numeral words, the *three* fires are well enough known even at the present day in India. Hence we get 873 or A.D. 1753, as above.

[*To follow Table I.*]

As the above tables are given by way of supplement to the results tabulated in the Historical Introduction to my Catalogue, I take this opportunity of offering a few remarks on some points touched on in the criticisms[1] that have appeared on that work, and likewise of calling attention to several passages in the work in general, to which my notice has been directed from these and from other sources.

And first as regards the Historical or, as I perhaps might have called it, the Chronological Introduction. Dr Oldenberg thinks that my remarks (Catalogue, p. vi sqq.) on the relation of the dates given in the MSS. to the native chronicles and to the dates given by Kirkpatrick are somewhat infelicitous, in that I had "evidently not at all, or only unconnectedly, made such researches as might have given clear insight into the origin and value of the earlier Nepalese tradition."

I am not at all sure that detailed criticism of the Vaṃçāvalī would have formed a legitimate part of a library catalogue, the object of which seems to me rather to provide material for research than to originate theories. Be this as it may, the necessity for the critical investigation of the period before 1000 A.D. was to a great extent rendered unnecessary by the promise, to which I referred at p. xli, of a sequel to the article by Drs Bhagvānlāl and Bühler in the *Indian Antiquary* for August 1880. This has now appeared in the same journal for December 1884[2] and deals with the relation of the Vaṃçāvalī to the inscriptions down to the IXth century, the writers being pleased to consider my treatment of the period covered by the later group of inscriptions so "carefully worked out" as to render further notice unnecessary. This being so, I am still somewhat at a loss,—though I have, I hope, sufficiently pondered on Dr Oldenberg's strictures,—to know what precisely are the available

[1] See the *Athenæum* for 15 Sept. 1883; *Academy* for 30 August 1884 (vol. 26, p. 140) (Prof. T. W. Rhys Davids); *Deutsche Litteraturzeitung*, 22 Dec. 1883 (Dr H. Oldenberg); *Göttingische Gelehrte Anzeigen* 18 Sept. 1885 (Prof. Th. Zachariae); *Litterarisches Centralblatt* 21 March 1885, [Prof. E.] Wi[ndisch]; *Journal Asiatique*, Jan. 1886 (M. L. Feer).

[2] The present co-editor, Mr Fleet, has now published another paper on this subject, in the number for December 1885, as noted at p. 72 above.

materials for the critical '*Untersuchungen*' that he would have me institute.

As for documentary material, I have made some use for the present publication of a manuscript of the Vaṃçāvalī, as already stated (page 16, note); but I find that its differences from the text translated by Dr Wright consist almost entirely in the omission of a few of the legendary and anecdotal passages of that work. Some differences, indeed, of assigned lengths of reign there are, and these have been registered in the columns of the Table of Kings (under "Gorkha histories"); but the tradition is clearly the same. As to its value I agree with Pandit Bhagvānlāl that "Dr Wright's data are on the whole trustworthy," and I think that the new matter I have now brought to light tends to give remarkable confirmation of these native records which are not to be so lightly set aside as some critics would have us believe. This applies also to a date (A.D. 1141) noted by me at Paris, in the Hodgson collection of the Bibliothèque Nationale, while passing the present work through the press. Though of little importance in itself, it is satisfactory to observe how well this date accords with the periods assigned by me from the Vaṃçāvalī for the adjacent reigns. See Table I.

Some difficulties, such as the date A.D. 1662, remarked on in the note to Table II., do no doubt occur even in comparatively recent times; yet on the other hand, as has been before pointed out, we find the tradition preserved, somewhat confusedly it is true, but still unmistakeably, of an interesting event like the establishment of the Çrīharsha era[1].

In the present work I have occasionally (as at pp. 8—9) ventured on a historical conjecture or tentative correction of the Vaṃçāvalī, which may be taken for what it is worth till further historical material comes to hand.

What the particular origin (*Herkunft*) of the Nepalese Vaṃçāvalī may be, I have no means of knowing, and should be glad to learn anything to supplement the statements of Dr Wright and Pandit Bhagvānlāl on the subject.

[1] See Wright pp. 131—2 and 134, cited in my Catalogue p. xli *et alibi*.

Dr Windisch, in the course of a courteous and detailed notice, thinks my description of the Mahāvastu too lengthy, because I "knew that it would be edited by M. Sénart." I was indeed aware that he had begun it, but as to when it may be finished I have no information.

I am indebted to the same reviewer for corrections of my reading of the colophon of Add. 1643 (pp. 151—2).

As to the last two corrections, the former, *sanāttanāṃm* (for p. 152, l. 5), I am afraid I do not fully understand. The latter, *samvatsare* for *samvatso*, is merely typographical and had appeared in the corrigenda of the catalogue, opposite page 1.

On page 178, l. 2, I must decline to accept Dr Windisch's *praṇāça* for *praṇāla*. The verses in question deal with the supply of water, and in a well-irrigated country like Nepal the *praṇāli* or *praṇāla* (conduit) plays an important part. The word occurs in various forms both in Dr Bhagvānlāl's inscriptions and in those now published.

My friend Pandit Durgāprasāda of Jeypore, who manifested an interest that quite surprised me in a literature new to him, was good enough to read through a considerable part of my catalogue and favoured me with several emendations, which I have found on comparing them with the originals at Cambridge to be quite correct.

I have to thank all my critics for the appreciative way in which they have treated my palæographic essay; and it is some satisfaction to note that Professor Bühler, in his Appendix to Professor Max Müller's and Bunyiu Nanjio's "Ancient Palm-leaves from Japan" has followed precisely the same lines with frequent references to our earliest MSS.

On merely palæographic grounds I confess I was not at all surprised to find doubts expressed, like those of Professor Beal in the *Athenæum*, July 4th, 1885, as to the very early date assigned to those palm-leaves. The fact is that, as was pointed out in the review of Professor Max Müller's publication in the same journal for October 4th, 1884, the balance of archaism in forms of letters is, even on Professor Bühler's showing, rather in favour of the Cambridge MS., e.g. in the form of य.

I now subjoin the list of corrections that I have been able to make from these and other sources.

Page vi, line 6, for 1065, read 1039.

„ 29, „ 14, 15, for °चरणांब्जधूलिध्वसराणां read °णाब्ज-धूलिधू°.

Page 32, „ 8, for शक्नुवन्ति read शंकुचन्ति [i.e. संकु°].

„ „ „ 11, for पदस्य read पादस्य.

„ 82, „ 14, 15, for परार्द्धां...नितचारु° read परार्ध्यां... सित°.

Page 93, last line, for Add. 1164 read Add. 1161.

„ 157, last line but one, for [सुपि] read [स्वि] and dele (*sic*).

„ 175, line 4, for 11—117 read 11—84, 84*, 85—117.

„ 182, „ 2, „ 1694 read 1691. 4.

Index, p. 210, col. 2. Add cross-reference: Laṅkāvatāra, see Saddharma-laṅkāvatāra.

P. 211, col. 1 and 222, col. 2. } Under Saddharma-laṅkāv° add a reference to p. 20.

P. 212. Add a reference to Sarvajñamitra of Kashmir, p. 29.

P. 217, col. 1, line 10. For 104 read 106.

The use of *piṭaka* at p. 21, l. 3 seems also to merit insertion in Index III.

INDEX.

This index chiefly deals with the names of persons and of places visited. The titles of MSS. (not the names of their authors) are also included, and printed in italics, in cases where some special notice or citation is given in the text.

UNIVERSITY PRESS, CAMBRIDGE.
May, 1886.

CATALOGUE OF

WORKS

PUBLISHED FOR THE SYNDICS

OF THE

Cambridge University Press.

London: C. J. CLAY AND SON,
CAMBRIDGE UNIVERSITY PRESS WAREHOUSE,
AVE MARIA LANE.
GLASGOW: 263, ARGYLE STREET.

Cambridge: DEIGHTON, BELL AND CO.
Leipzig: F. A. BROCKHAUS.

5000
1/5/86

BREVIARIUM AD USUM INSIGNIS ECCLESIAE SARUM. Juxta Editionem maximam pro CLAUDIO CHEVALLON ET FRANCISCO REGNAULT A.D. MDXXXI. in Alma Parisiorum Academia impressam: labore ac studio FRANCISCI PROCTER, A.M., ET CHRISTOPHORI WORDSWORTH, A.M.

FASCICULUS I. In quo continentur KALENDARIUM, et ORDO TEMPORALIS sive PROPRIUM DE TEMPORE TOTIUS ANNI, una cum ordinali suo quod usitato vocabulo dicitur PICA SIVE DIRECTORIUM SACERDOTUM. Demy 8vo. 18*s*.

"The value of this reprint is considerable to liturgical students, who will now be able to consult in their own libraries a work absolutely indispensable to a right understanding of the history of the Prayer-Book, but which till now usually necessitated a visit to some public library, since the rarity of the volume made its cost prohibitory to all but a few.... Messrs Procter and Wordsworth have discharged their editorial task with much care and judgment, though the conditions under which they have been working are such as to hide that fact from all but experts."—*Literary Churchman.*

FASCICULUS II. In quo continentur PSALTERIUM, cum ordinario Officii totius hebdomadae juxta Horas Canonicas, et proprio Completorii, LITANIA, COMMUNE SANCTORUM, ORDINARIUM MISSAE CUM CANONE ET XIII MISSIS, &c. &c. Demy 8vo. 12*s*.

"Not only experts in liturgiology, but all persons interested in the history of the Anglican Book of Common Prayer, will be grateful to the Syndicate of the Cambridge University Press for forwarding the publication of the volume which bears the above title, and which has recently appeared under their auspices."—*Notes and Queries.*

"Cambridge has worthily taken the lead with the Breviary, which is of especial value for that part of the reform of the Prayer-Book which will fit it for the wants of our time... For all persons of religious tastes the Breviary, with its mixture of Psalm and Anthem and Prayer and Hymn, all hanging one on the other, and connected into a harmonious whole, must be deeply interesting."—*Church Quarterly Review.*

"The editors have done their work excellently, and deserve all praise for their labours in rendering what they justly call 'this most interesting Service-book' more readily accessible to historical and liturgical students."—*Saturday Review.*

FASCICULUS III. In quo continetur PROPRIUM SANCTORUM quod et sanctorale dicitur, una cum accentuario. [*Nearly ready.*

GREEK AND ENGLISH TESTAMENT, in parallel Columns on the same page. Edited by J. SCHOLEFIELD, M.A. late Regius Professor of Greek in the University. Small Octavo. New Edition, with the Marginal References as arranged and revised by Dr SCRIVENER. Cloth, red edges. 7*s*. 6*d*.

GREEK AND ENGLISH TESTAMENT. THE STUDENT'S EDITION of the above, on *large writing paper*. 4to. 12*s*.

GREEK TESTAMENT, ex editione Stephani tertia, 1550. Small 8vo. 3*s*. 6*d*.

THE NEW TESTAMENT IN GREEK according to the text followed in the Authorised Version, with the Variations adopted in the Revised Version. Edited by F. H. A. SCRIVENER, M.A., D.C.L., LL.D. Crown 8vo. 6*s*. Morocco boards or limp. 12*s*.

THE PARALLEL NEW TESTAMENT GREEK AND ENGLISH, being the Authorised Version set forth in 1611 Arranged in Parallel Columns with the Revised Version of 1881, and with the original Greek, as edited by F. H. A. SCRIVENER, M.A., D.C.L., LL.D. Prebendary of Exeter and Vicar of Hendon. Crown 8vo. 12*s*. 6*d*. *The Revised Version is the Joint Property of the Universities of Cambridge and Oxford.*

London: C. J. CLAY & SON, Cambridge University Press Warehouse, Ave Maria Lane.

THE BOOK OF ECCLESIASTES, with Notes and Introduction. By the Very Rev. E. H. PLUMPTRE, D.D., Dean of Wells. Large Paper Edition. Demy 8vo. 7*s.* 6*d.*

"No one can say that the Old Testament is a dull or worn-out subject after reading this singularly attractive and also instructive commentary. Its wealth of literary and historical illustration surpasses anything to which we can point in English exegesis of the Old Testament; indeed, even Delitzsch, whose pride it is to leave no source of illustration unexplored, is far inferior on this head to Dr Plumptre."—*Academy*, Sept. 10, 1881.

THE GOSPEL ACCORDING TO ST MATTHEW in Anglo-Saxon and Northumbrian Versions, synoptically arranged: with Collations of the best Manuscripts. By J. M. KEMBLE, M.A. and Archdeacon HARDWICK. Demy 4to. 10*s.*

NEW EDITION. By the Rev. Professor SKEAT. [*In the Press.*

THE GOSPEL ACCORDING TO ST MARK in Anglo-Saxon and Northumbrian Versions, synoptically arranged: with Collations exhibiting all the Readings of all the MSS. Edited by the Rev. W. W. SKEAT, M.A. Elrington and Bosworth Professor of Anglo-Saxon. Demy 4to. 10*s.*

THE GOSPEL ACCORDING TO ST LUKE, uniform with the preceding, by the same Editor. Demy 4to. 10*s.*

THE GOSPEL ACCORDING TO ST JOHN, uniform with the preceding, by the same Editor. Demy 4to. 10*s.*

"*The Gospel according to St John, in Anglo-Saxon and Northumbrian Versions:* Edited for the Syndics of the University Press, by the Rev. Walter W. Skeat, M.A., completes an undertaking designed and commenced by that distinguished scholar, J. M. Kemble, some forty years ago. Of the particular volume now before us, we can only say it is worthy of its two predecessors. We repeat that the service rendered to the study of Anglo-Saxon by this Synoptic collection cannot easily be overstated."—*Contemporary Review.*

THE POINTED PRAYER BOOK, being the Book of Common Prayer with the Psalter or Psalms of David, pointed as they are to be sung or said in Churches. Royal 24mo. 1*s.* 6*d.*

The same in square 32mo. cloth. 6*d.*

THE CAMBRIDGE PSALTER, for the use of Choirs and Organists. Specially adapted for Congregations in which the "Cambridge Pointed Prayer Book" is used. Demy 8vo. cloth extra, 3*s.* 6*d.* cloth limp, cut flush. 2*s.* 6*d.*

THE PARAGRAPH PSALTER, arranged for the use of Choirs by BROOKE FOSS WESTCOTT, D.D., Regius Professor of Divinity in the University of Cambridge. Fcap. 4to. 5*s.*

The same in royal 32mo. Cloth 1*s.* Leather 1*s.* 6*d.*

"The Paragraph Psalter exhibits all the care, thought, and learning that those acquainted with the works of the Regius Professor of Divinity at Cambridge would expect to find, and there is not a clergyman or organist in England who should be without this Psalter as a work of reference."—*Morning Post.*

THE MISSING FRAGMENT OF THE LATIN TRANSLATION OF THE FOURTH BOOK OF EZRA, discovered, and edited with an Introduction and Notes, and a facsimile of the MS., by ROBERT L. BENSLY, M.A., Reader in Hebrew, Gonville and Caius College, Cambridge. Demy 4to. 10*s.*

"It has been said of this book that it has added a new chapter to the Bible, and, startling as the statement may at first sight appear, it is no exaggeration of the actual fact, if by the Bible we understand that of the larger size which contains the Apocrypha, and if the Second Book of Esdras can be fairly called a part of the Apocrypha."—*Saturday Review.*

GOSPEL DIFFICULTIES, or the Displaced Section of S. Luke. By the Rev. J. J. HALCOMBE, Rector of Balsham and Rural Dean of North Camps, formerly Reader and Librarian at the Charterhouse. Crown 8vo. 10*s.* 6*d.*

THEOLOGY—(ANCIENT).

THE GREEK LITURGIES. Chiefly from original Authorities. By C. A. SWAINSON, D.D., Master of Christ's College, Cambridge. Crown 4to. Paper covers. 15*s*.

"Jeder folgende Forscher wird dankbar anerkennen, dass Swainson das Fundament zu einer historisch-kritischen Geschichte der Griechischen Liturgien sicher gelegt hat."—ADOLPH HARNACK, *Theologische Literatur-Zeitung*.

THE PALESTINIAN MISHNA. By W. H. LOWE, M.A., Lecturer in Hebrew at Christ's College, Cambridge. Royal 8vo. 21*s*.

SAYINGS OF THE JEWISH FATHERS, comprising Pirqe Aboth and Pereq R. Meir in Hebrew and English, with Critical and Illustrative Notes. By CHARLES TAYLOR, D.D. Master of St John's College, Cambridge, and Honorary Fellow of King's College, London. Demy 8vo. 10*s*.

"The 'Masseketh Aboth' stands at the head of Hebrew non-canonical writings. It is of ancient date, claiming to contain the dicta of teachers who flourished from B.C. 200 to the same year of our era. The precise time of its compilation in its present form is, of course, in doubt. Mr Taylor's explanatory and illustrative commentary is very full and satisfactory."—*Spectator*.

"A careful and thorough edition which does credit to English scholarship, of a short treatise from the Mishna, containing a series of sentences or maxims ascribed mostly to Jewish teachers immediately preceding, or immediately following the Christian era. . ."—*Contemporary Review*.

THEODORE OF MOPSUESTIA'S COMMENTARY ON THE MINOR EPISTLES OF S. PAUL. The Latin Version with the Greek Fragments, edited from the MSS. with Notes and an Introduction, by H. B. SWETE, D.D., Rector of Ashdon, Essex, and late Fellow of Gonville and Caius College, Cambridge. In Two Volumes. Vol. I., containing the Introduction, with Facsimiles of the MSS., and the Commentary upon Galatians—Colossians. Demy 8vo. 12*s*.

"In dem oben verzeichneten Buche liegt uns die erste Hälfte einer vollständigen, ebenso sorgfältig gearbeiteten wie schön ausgestatteten Ausgabe des Commentars mit ausführlichen Prolegomena und reichhaltigen kritischen und erläuternden Anmerkungen vor."—*Literarisches Centralblatt*.

"It is the result of thorough, careful, and patient investigation of all the points bearing on the subject, and the results are presented with admirable good sense and modesty."—*Guardian*.

"Auf Grund dieser Quellen ist der Text bei Swete mit musterhafter Akribie hergestellt. Aber auch sonst hat der Herausgeber mit unermüdlichem Fleisse und eingehendster Sachkenntniss sein Werk mit allen denjenigen Zugaben ausgerüstet, welche bei einer solchen Text-Ausgabe nur irgend erwartet werden können. . . . Von den drei Haupthandschriften . . . sind vortreffliche photographische Facsimile's beigegeben, wie überhaupt das ganze Werk von der *University Press* zu Cambridge mit bekannter Eleganz ausgestattet ist."—*Theologische Literaturzeitung*.

"It is a hopeful sign, amid forebodings which arise about the theological learning of the Universities, that we have before us the first instalment of a thoroughly scientific and painstaking work, commenced at Cambridge and completed at a country rectory."—*Church Quarterly Review* (Jan. 1881).

"Hernn Swete's Leistung ist eine so tüchtige dass wir das Werk in keinen besseren Händen wissen möchten, und mit den sichersten Erwartungen auf das Gelingen der Fortsetzung entgegen sehen."—*Göttingische gelehrte Anzeigen* (Sept. 1881).

VOLUME II., containing the Commentary on 1 Thessalonians—Philemon, Appendices and Indices. 12*s*.

"Eine Ausgabe . . . für welche alle zugänglichen Hülfsmittel in musterhafter Weise benützt wurden . . . eine reife Frucht siebenjährigen Fleisses."—*Theologische Literaturzeitung* (Sept. 23, 1882).

"Mit deiselben Sorgfalt bearbeitet die wir bei dem ersten Theile gerühmt haben."—*Literarisches Centralblatt* (July 29, 1882).

"M. Jacobi...commença...une édition du texte. Ce travail a été repris en Angleterre et mené à bien dans les deux volumes que je signale en ce moment...Elle est accompagnée de notes érudites, suivie de divers appendices, parmi lesquels on appréciera surtout un recueil des fragments des oeuvres dogmatiques de Théodore, et précédée d'une introduction où sont traitées à fond toutes les questions d'histoire littéraire qui se rattachent soit au commentaire lui-même, soit à sa version Latine."—*Bulletin Critique*, 1885.

SANCTI IRENÆI EPISCOPI LUGDUNENSIS libros quinque adversus Hæreses, versione Latina cum Codicibus Claromontano ac Arundeliano denuo collata, præmissa de placitis Gnosticorum prolusione, fragmenta necnon Græce, Syriace, Armeniace, commentatione perpetua et indicibus variis edidit W. WIGAN HARVEY, S.T.B. Collegii Regalis olim Socius. 2 Vols. 8vo. 18*s.*

M. MINUCII FELICIS OCTAVIUS. The text newly revised from the original MS., with an English Commentary, Analysis, Introduction, and Copious Indices. Edited by H. A. HOLDEN, LL.D. late Fellow of Trinity College. Crown 8vo. 7*s.* 6*d.*

THEOPHILI EPISCOPI ANTIOCHENSIS LIBRI TRES AD AUTOLYCUM edidit, Prolegomenis Versione Notulis Indicibus instruxit GULIELMUS GILSON HUMPHRY, S.T.B. Collegii Sanctiss. Trin. apud Cantabrigienses quondam Socius. Post 8vo. 5*s.*

THEOPHYLACTI IN EVANGELIUM S. MATTHÆI COMMENTARIUS, edited by W. G. HUMPHRY, B.D. Prebendary of St Paul's, late Fellow of Trinity College. Demy 8vo. 7*s.* 6*d.*

TERTULLIANUS DE CORONA MILITIS, DE SPECTACULIS, DE IDOLOLATRIA, with Analysis and English Notes, by GEORGE CURREY, D.D. Preacher at the Charter House, late Fellow and Tutor of St John's College. Crown 8vo. 5*s.*

THEOLOGY—(ENGLISH).

WORKS OF ISAAC BARROW, compared with the Original MSS., enlarged with Materials hitherto unpublished. A new Edition, by A. NAPIER, M.A. of Trinity College, Vicar of Holkham, Norfolk. 9 Vols. Demy 8vo. £3. 3*s.*

TREATISE OF THE POPE'S SUPREMACY, and a Discourse concerning the Unity of the Church, by ISAAC BARROW. Demy 8vo. 7*s.* 6*d.*

PEARSON'S EXPOSITION OF THE CREED, edited by TEMPLE CHEVALLIER, B.D. late Fellow and Tutor of St Catharine's College, Cambridge. New Edition. Revised by R. Sinker, B.D., Librarian of Trinity College. Demy 8vo. 12*s.*

"A new edition of Bishop Pearson's famous work *On the Creed* has just been issued by the Cambridge University Press. It is the well-known edition of Temple Chevallier, thoroughly overhauled by the Rev. R. Sinker, of Trinity College. The whole text and notes have been most carefully examined and corrected, and special pains have been taken to verify the almost innumerable references. These have been more clearly and accurately given in very many places, and the citations themselves have been adapted to the best and newest texts of the several authors—texts which have undergone vast improvements within the last two centuries. The Indices have also been revised and enlarged......Altogether this appears to be the most complete and convenient edition as yet published of a work which has long been recognised in all quarters as a standard one."—*Guardian.*

AN ANALYSIS OF THE EXPOSITION OF THE CREED written by the Right Rev. JOHN PEARSON, D.D. late Lord Bishop of Chester, by W. H. MILL, D.D. late Regius Professor of Hebrew in the University of Cambridge. Demy 8vo. 5*s.*

WHEATLY ON THE COMMON PRAYER, edited by G. E. CORRIE, D.D. late Master of Jesus College, Examining Chaplain to the late Lord Bishop of Ely. Demy 8vo. 7*s.* 6*d.*

TWO FORMS OF PRAYER OF THE TIME OF QUEEN ELIZABETH. Now First Reprinted. Demy 8vo. *6d.*

"From 'Collections and Notes' 1867—1876, by W. Carew Hazlitt (p. 340), we learn that—'A very remarkable volume, in the original vellum cover, and containing 25 Forms of Prayer of the reign of Elizabeth, each with the autograph of Humphrey Dyson, has lately fallen into the hands of my friend Mr H. Pyne. It is mentioned specially in the Preface to the Parker Society's volume of Occasional Forms of Prayer, but it had been lost sight of for 200 years.' By the kindness of the present possessor of this valuable volume, containing in all 25 distinct publications, I am enabled to reprint in the following pages the two Forms of Prayer supposed to have been lost."—*Extract from the* PREFACE.

CÆSAR MORGAN'S INVESTIGATION OF THE TRINITY OF PLATO, and of Philo Judæus, and of the effects which an attachment to their writings had upon the principles and reasonings of the Fathers of the Christian Church. Revised by H. A. HOLDEN, LL.D., formerly Fellow of Trinity College, Cambridge. Crown 8vo. *4s.*

SELECT DISCOURSES, by JOHN SMITH, late Fellow of Queens' College, Cambridge. Edited by H. G. WILLIAMS, B.D. late Professor of Arabic. Royal 8vo. *7s. 6d.*

"The 'Select Discourses' of John Smith, collected and published from his papers after his death, are, in my opinion, much the most considerable work left to us by this Cambridge School [the Cambridge Platonists]. They have a right to a place in English literary history."—Mr MATTHEW ARNOLD, in the *Contemporary Review.*

"Of all the products of the Cambridge School, the 'Select Discourses' are perhaps the highest, as they are the most accessible and the most widely appreciated...and indeed no spiritually thoughtful mind can read them unmoved. They carry us so directly into an atmosphere of divine philosophy, luminous with the richest lights of meditative genius... He was one of those rare thinkers in whom largeness of view, and depth, and wealth of poetic and speculative insight, only served to evoke more fully the religious spirit, and while he drew the mould of his thought from Plotinus, he vivified the substance of it from St Paul."—Principal TULLOCH, *Rational Theology in England in the 17th Century.*

"We may instance Mr Henry Griffin Williams's revised edition of Mr John Smith's 'Select Discourses,' which have won Mr Matthew Arnold's admiration, as an example of worthy work for an University Press to undertake."—*Times.*

THE HOMILIES, with Various Readings, and the Quotations from the Fathers given at length in the Original Languages. Edited by G. E. CORRIE, D.D. late Master of Jesus College. Demy 8vo. *7s. 6d.*

DE OBLIGATIONE CONSCIENTIÆ PRÆLECTIONES decem Oxonii in Schola Theologica habitæ a ROBERTO SANDERSON, SS. Theologiæ ibidem Professore Regio. With English Notes, including an abridged Translation, by W. WHEWELL, D.D. late Master of Trinity College. Demy 8vo. *7s. 6d.*

ARCHBISHOP USHER'S ANSWER TO A JESUIT, with other Tracts on Popery. Edited by J. SCHOLEFIELD, M.A. late Regius Professor of Greek in the University. Demy 8vo. *7s. 6d.*

WILSON'S ILLUSTRATION OF THE METHOD OF explaining the New Testament, by the early opinions of Jews and Christians concerning Christ. Edited by T. TURTON, D.D. late Lord Bishop of Ely. Demy 8vo. *5s.*

LECTURES ON DIVINITY delivered in the University of Cambridge, by JOHN HEY, D.D. Third Edition, revised by T. TURTON, D.D. late Lord Bishop of Ely. 2 vols. Demy 8vo. *15s.*

ARABIC, SANSKRIT, SYRIAC, &c.

THE DIVYÂVADÂNA, a Collection of Early Buddhist Legends, now first edited from the Nepalese Sanskrit MSS. in Cambridge and Paris. By E. B. COWELL, M.A., Professor of Sanskrit in the University of Cambridge, and R. A. NEIL, M.A., Fellow and Lecturer of Pembroke College. Demy 8vo. 18*s.*

POEMS OF BEHA ED DIN ZOHEIR OF EGYPT. With a Metrical Translation, Notes and Introduction, by E. H. PALMER, M.A., Barrister-at-Law of the Middle Temple, late Lord Almoner's Professor of Arabic, formerly Fellow of St John's College, Cambridge. 2 vols. Crown 4to.

Vol. I. The ARABIC TEXT. 10*s.* 6*d.*; cloth extra. 15*s.*
Vol. II. ENGLISH TRANSLATION. 10*s.* 6*d.*; cloth extra. 15*s.*

"We have no hesitation in saying that in both Prof. Palmer has made an addition to Oriental literature for which scholars should be grateful; and that, while his knowledge of Arabic is a sufficient guarantee for his mastery of the original, his English compositions are distinguished by versatility, command of language, rhythmical cadence, and, as we have remarked, by not unskilful imitations of the styles of several of our own favourite poets, living and dead."—*Saturday Review.*

"This sumptuous edition of the poems of Behá-ed-dín Zoheir is a very welcome addition to the small series of Eastern poets accessible to readers who are not Orientalists."—*Academy.*

THE CHRONICLE OF JOSHUA THE STYLITE, composed in Syriac A.D. 507 with an English translation and notes, by W. WRIGHT, LL.D., Professor of Arabic. Demy 8vo. 10*s.* 6*d.*

"Die lehrreiche kleine Chronik Josuas hat nach Assemani und Martin in Wright einen dritten Bearbeiter gefunden, der sich um die Emendation des Textes wie um die Erklärung der Realien wesentlich verdient gemacht hat . . . Ws. Josua-Ausgabe ist eine sehr dankenswerte Gabe und besonders empfehlenswert als ein Lehrmittel für den syrischen Unterricht; es erscheint auch gerade zur rechten Zeit, da die zweite Ausgabe von Roedigers syrischer Chrestomathie im Buchhandel vollständig vergriffen und diejenige von Kirsch-Bernstein nur noch in wenigen Exemplaren vorhanden ist."—*Deutsche Litteraturzeitung.*

KALĪLAH AND DIMNAH, OR, THE FABLES OF BIDPAI; being an account of their literary history, together with an English Translation of the same, with Notes, by I. G. N. KEITH-FALCONER, M.A., Trinity College. Demy 8vo. 7*s.* 6*d*

NALOPÂKHYÂNAM, OR, THE TALE OF NALA; containing the Sanskrit Text in Roman Characters, followed by a Vocabulary and a sketch of Sanskrit Grammar. By the late Rev. THOMAS JARRETT, M.A. Trinity College, Regius Professor of Hebrew. Demy 8vo. 10*s.*

NOTES ON THE TALE OF NALA, for the use of Classical Students, by J. PEILE, Litt.D., Fellow and Tutor of Christ's College. Demy 8vo. 12*s.*

CATALOGUE OF THE BUDDHIST SANSKRIT MANUSCRIPTS in the University Library, Cambridge. Edited by C. BENDALL, M.A., Fellow of Gonville and Caius College. Demy 8vo. 12*s.*

"It is unnecessary to state how the compilation of the present catalogue came to be placed in Mr Bendall's hands: from the character of his work it is evident the selection was judicious, and we may fairly congratulate those concerned in it on the result . . . Mr Bendall has entitled himself to the thanks of all Oriental scholars, and we hope he may have before him a long course of successful labour in the field he has chosen."—*Athenæum.*

GREEK AND LATIN CLASSICS, &c.

SOPHOCLES: The Plays and Fragments, with Critical Notes, Commentary, and Translation in English Prose, by R. C. JEBB, Litt.D., LL.D., Professor of Greek in the University of Glasgow.

Part I. Oedipus Tyrannus. Demy 8vo. 15*s*.

Part II. Oedipus Coloneus. Demy 8vo. 12*s*. 6*d*.

"Of his explanatory and critical notes we can only speak with admiration. Thorough scholarship combines with taste, erudition, and boundless industry to make this first volume a pattern of editing. The work is made complete by a prose translation, upon pages alternating with the text, of which we may say shortly that it displays sound judgment and taste, without sacrificing precision to poetry of expression."—*The Times*.

"This larger edition he has deferred these many years for reasons which he has given in his preface, and which we accept with entire satisfaction, as we have now the first portion of a work composed in the fulness of his powers and with all the resources of fine erudition and laboriously earned experience...We will confidently aver, then, that the edition is neither tedious nor long; for we get in one compact volume such a cyclopædia of instruction, such a variety of helps to the full comprehension of the poet, as not so many years ago would have needed a small library, and all this instruction and assistance given, not in a dull and pedantic way, but in a style of singular clearness and vivacity. In fact, one might take this edition with him on a journey, and, without any other help whatever, acquire with comfort and delight a thorough acquaintance with the noblest production of, perhaps, the most difficult of all Greek poets—the most difficult, yet possessed at the same time of an immortal charm for one who has mastered him, as Mr Jebb has, and can feel so subtly perfection of form and language...We await with lively expectation the continuation, and completion of Mr Jebb's great task, and it is a fortunate thing that his power of work seems to be as great as the style is happy in which the work is done."—*The Athenæum*.

"An edition which marks a definite advance, which is whole in itself, and brings a mass of solid and well-wrought material such as future constructors will desire to adapt, is definitive in the only applicable sense of the term, and such is the edition of Professor Jebb. No man is better fitted to express in relation to Sophocles the mind of the present generation."—*The Saturday Review*.

AESCHYLI FABULAE.—ΙΚΕΤΙΔΕΣ ΧΟΗΦΟΡΟΙ IN LIBRO MEDICEO MENDOSE SCRIPTAE EX VV. DD. CONIECTURIS EMENDATIUS EDITAE cum Scholiis Graecis et brevi adnotatione critica, curante F. A. PALEY, M.A., LL.D. Demy 8vo. 7*s*. 6*d*.

THE AGAMEMNON OF AESCHYLUS. With a Translation in English Rhythm, and Notes Critical and Explanatory. **New Edition Revised.** By BENJAMIN HALL KENNEDY, D.D., Regius Professor of Greek. Crown 8vo. 6*s*.

"One of the best editions of the masterpiece of Greek tragedy."—*Athenæum*.

THE THEÆTETUS OF PLATO with a Translation and Notes by the same Editor. Crown 8vo. 7*s*. 6*d*.

ARISTOTLE.—ΠΕΡΙ ΨΥΧΗΣ. ARISTOTLE'S PSYCHOLOGY, in Greek and English, with Introduction and Notes, by EDWIN WALLACE, M.A., late Fellow and Tutor of Worcester College, Oxford. Demy 8vo. 18*s*.

"The notes are exactly what such notes ought to be,—helps to the student, not mere displays of learning. By far the more valuable parts of the notes are neither critical nor literary, but philosophical and expository of the thought, and of the connection of thought, in the treatise itself. In this relation the notes are invaluable. Of the translation, it may be said that an English reader may fairly master by means of it this great treatise of Aristotle."—*Spectator*.

"Wallace's Bearbeitung der Aristotelischen Psychologie ist das Werk eines denkenden und in allen Schriften des Aristoteles und grösstenteils auch in der neueren Litteratur zu denselben belesenen Mannes... Der schwächste Teil der Arbeit ist der kritische... Aber in allen diesen Dingen liegt auch nach der Absicht des Verfassers nicht der Schwerpunkt seiner Arbeit, sondern."—Prof. Susemihl in *Philologische Wochenschrift*.

ARISTOTLE.—ΠΕΡΙ ΔΙΚΑΙΟΣΥΝΗΣ. THE FIFTH BOOK OF THE NICOMACHEAN ETHICS OF ARISTOTLE. Edited by HENRY JACKSON, Litt.D., Fellow of Trinity College, Cambridge. Demy 8vo. 6*s*.

"It is not too much to say that some of the points he discusses have never had so much light thrown upon them before.... Scholars will hope that this is not the only portion of the Aristotelian writings which he is likely to edit."—*Athenæum*.

ARISTOTLE. THE RHETORIC. With a Commentary by the late E. M. COPE, Fellow of Trinity College, Cambridge, revised and edited by J. E. SANDYS, M.A. With a biographical Memoir by the late H. A. J. MUNRO, Litt. D. 3 Vols., Demy 8vo. **Now reduced to 21s.** *(originally published at 31s. 6d.)*

"This work is in many ways creditable to the University of Cambridge. If an English student wishes to have a full conception of what is contained in the *Rhetoric* of Aristotle, to Mr Cope's edition he must go."—*Academy.*

"Mr Sandys has performed his arduous duties with marked ability and admirable tact. . . . . . In every part of his work—revising, supplementing, and completing—he has done exceedingly well."—*Examiner.*

PINDAR. OLYMPIAN AND PYTHIAN ODES. With Notes Explanatory and Critical, Introductions and Introductory Essays. Edited by C. A. M. FENNELL, Litt. D., late Fellow of Jesus College. Crown 8vo. 9s.

"Mr Fennell deserves the thanks of all classical students for his careful and scholarly edition of the Olympian and Pythian odes. He brings to his task the necessary enthusiasm for his author, great industry, a sound judgment, and, in particular, copious and minute learning in comparative philology."—*Athenæum.*

"Considered simply as a contribution to the study and criticism of Pindar, Mr Fennell's edition is a work of great merit."—*Saturday Review.*

—— **THE ISTHMIAN AND NEMEAN ODES.** By the same Editor. Crown 8vo. 9s.

". . . As a handy and instructive edition of a difficult classic no work of recent years surpasses Mr Fennell's 'Pindar.'"—*Athenæum.*

"This work is in no way inferior to the previous volume. The commentary affords valuable help to the study of the most difficult of Greek authors, and is enriched with notes on points of scholarship and etymology which could only have been written by a scholar of very high attainments."—*Saturday Review.*

PRIVATE ORATIONS OF DEMOSTHENES, with Introductions and English Notes, by F. A. PALEY, M.A. Editor of Aeschylus, etc. and J. E. SANDYS, M.A. Fellow and Tutor of St John's College, and Public Orator in the University of Cambridge.

PART I. Contra Phormionem, Lacritum, Pantaenetum, Boeotum de Nomine, Boeotum de Dote, Dionysodorum. Crown 8vo. 6s.

[*New Edition. In the Press.*

"Mr Paley's scholarship is sound and accurate, his experience of editing wide, and if he is content to devote his learning and abilities to the production of such manuals as these, they will be received with gratitude throughout the higher schools of the country. Mr Sandys is deeply read in the German literature which bears upon his author, and the elucidation of matters of daily life, in the delineation of which Demosthenes is so rich, obtains full justice at his hands. . . . We hope this edition may lead the way to a more general study of these speeches in schools than has hitherto been possible."—*Academy.*

PART II. Pro Phormione, Contra Stephanum I. II.; Nicostratum, Cononem, Calliclem. Crown 8vo. 7s. 6d.

"It is long since we have come upon a work evincing more pains, scholarship, and varied research and illustration than Mr Sandys's contribution to the 'Private Orations of Demosthenes'."—*Saturday Review.*

". . . . . . the edition reflects credit on Cambridge scholarship, and ought to be extensively used."—*Athenæum.*

DEMOSTHENES AGAINST ANDROTION AND AGAINST TIMOCRATES, with Introductions and English Commentary, by WILLIAM WAYTE, M.A., late Professor of Greek, University College, London. Crown 8vo. 7s. 6d.

"These speeches are highly interesting, as illustrating Attic Law, as that law was influenced by the exigences of politics . . . As vigorous examples of the great orator's style, they are worthy of all admiration; and they have the advantage—not inconsiderable when the actual attainments of the average schoolboy are considered—of having an easily comprehended subject matter . . . . Besides a most lucid and interesting introduction, Mr Wayte has given the student effective help in his running commentary. We may note, as being so well managed as to form a very valuable part of the exegesis, the summaries given with every two or three sections throughout the speech."—*Spectator.*

PLATO'S PHÆDO, literally translated, by the late E. M. COPE, Fellow of Trinity College, Cambridge, revised by HENRY JACKSON, Litt. D., Fellow of Trinity College. Demy 8vo. 5s.

THE BACCHAE OF EURIPIDES. With Introduction, Critical Notes, and Archæological Illustrations, by J. E. SANDYS, M.A., Fellow and Tutor of St John's College, Cambridge, and Public Orator. New and Enlarged Edition. Crown 8vo. 12*s*. 6*d*.

"Of the present edition of the *Bacchæ* by Mr Sandys we may safely say that never before has a Greek play, in England at least, had fuller justice done to its criticism, interpretation, and archæological illustration, whether for the young student or the more advanced scholar. The Cambridge Public Orator may be said to have taken the lead in issuing a complete edition of a Greek play, which is destined perhaps to gain redoubled favour now that the study of ancient monuments has been applied to its illustration."—*Saturday Review*.

"The volume is interspersed with well-executed woodcuts, and its general attractiveness of form reflects great credit on the University Press. In the notes Mr Sandys has more than sustained his well-earned reputation as a careful and learned editor, and shows considerable advance in freedom and lightness of style. . . . Under such circumstances it is superfluous to say that for the purposes of teachers and advanced students this handsome edition far surpasses all its predecessors."—*Athenæum*.

"It has not, like so many such books, been hastily produced to meet the momentary need of some particular examination; but it has employed for some years the labour and thought of a highly finished scholar, whose aim seems to have been that his book should go forth *totus teres atque rotundus*, armed at all points with all that may throw light upon its subject. The result is a work which will not only assist the schoolboy or undergraduate in his tasks, but will adorn the library of the scholar."—*The Guardian*.

THE TYPES OF GREEK COINS. By PERCY GARDNER, Litt. D., F.S.A., Disney Professor of Archæology. With 16 Autotype plates, containing photographs of Coins of all parts of the Greek World. Impl. 4to. Cloth extra, £1. 11*s*. 6*d*.; Roxburgh (Morocco back), £2. 2*s*.

"Professor Gardner's book is written with such lucidity and in a manner so straightforward that it may well win converts, and it may be distinctly recommended to that omnivorous class of readers—'men in the schools'."—*Saturday Review*.

"'The Types of Greek Coins' is a work which is less purely and dryly scientific. Nevertheless, it takes high rank as proceeding upon a truly scientific basis at the same time that it treats the subject of numismatics in an attractive style and is elegant enough to justify its appearance in the drawing-room."—*Athenæum*.

A SELECTION OF GREEK INSCRIPTIONS, with Introductions and Annotations by E. S. ROBERTS, M.A., Fellow and Tutor of Gonville and Caius College. [*In the Press*.

ESSAYS ON THE ART OF PHEIDIAS. By C. WALDSTEIN, M.A., Phil. D., Reader in Classical Archæology in the University of Cambridge. Royal 8vo. With numerous Illustrations. 16 Plates. Buckram, 30*s*.

"I acknowledge expressly the warm enthusiasm for ideal art which pervades the whole volume, and the sharp eye Dr Waldstein has proved himself to possess in his special line of study, namely, stylistic analysis, which has led him to several happy and important discoveries. His book will be universally welcomed as a very valuable contribution towards a more thorough knowledge of the style of Pheidias."—*The Academy*.

"'Essays on the Art of Pheidias' form an extremely valuable and important piece of work. . . . Taking it for the illustrations alone, it is an exceedingly facinating book."—*Times*.

M. TULLI CICERONIS AD. M. BRUTUM ORATOR. A revised text edited with Introductory Essays and with critical and explanatory notes, by J. E. SANDYS, M.A., Fellow and Tutor of St John's College, and Public Orator. Demy 8vo. 16*s*.

M. TULLI CICERONIS DE FINIBUS BONORUM ET MALORUM LIBRI QUINQUE. The text revised and explained; With a Translation by JAMES S. REID, Litt. D., Fellow and Tutor of Gonville and Caius College. 3 Vols. [*In the Press*.

VOL. III. Containing the Translation. Demy 8vo. 8*s*.

M. T. CICERONIS DE OFFICIIS LIBRI TRES, with Marginal Analysis, an English Commentary, and copious Indices, by H. A. HOLDEN, LL.D., late Fellow of Trinity College, Cambridge. **Sixth Edition,** Revised and Enlarged. Crown 8vo. 9*s*.

"Dr Holden has issued an edition of what is perhaps the easiest and most popular of Cicero's philosophical works, the *de Officiis*, which, especially in the form which it has now assumed after two most thorough revisions, leaves little or nothing to be desired in the fullness and accuracy of its treatment alike of the matter and the language."—*Academy*.

M. TVLLI CICERONIS PRO C RABIRIO [PERDVELLIONIS REO] ORATIO AD QVIRITES With Notes Introduction and Appendices by W. E. HEITLAND, M.A., Fellow and Tutor of St John's College, Cambridge. Demy 8vo. 7*s*. 6*d*.

M. TULLII CICERONIS DE NATURA DEORUM Libri Tres, with Introduction and Commentary by JOSEPH B. MAYOR, M.A., late Professor of Moral Philosophy at King's College, London, together with a new collation of several of the English MSS. by J. H. SWAINSON, M.A.

Vol. I. Demy 8vo. 10*s*. 6*d*. Vol. II. 12*s*. 6*d*. Vol. III. 10*s*.

"Such editions as that of which Prof. Mayor has given us the first instalment will doubtless do much to remedy this undeserved neglect. It is one on which great pains and much learning have evidently been expended, and is in every way admirably suited to meet the needs of the student . . . The notes of the editor are all that could be expected from his well-known learning and scholarship."—*Academy*.

"Der vorliegende zweite Band enthält N. D. II. und zeigt ebenso wie der erste einen erheblichen Fortschritt gegen die bisher vorhandenen commentirten Ausgaben. Man darf jetzt, nachdem der grösste Theil erschienen ist, sagen, dass niemand, welcher sich sachlich oder kritisch mit der Schrift De Nat. Deor. beschäftigt, die neue Ausgabe wird ignoriren dürfen."—P. SCHWENCKE in *JB. f. cl. Alt.* vol. 35, p. 90 foll.

"Nell' edizione sua è più compiuto, che in qualunque altra edizione anteriore, e in parte nuove, non meno l' apparato critico dal testo che l' esame ed il commento del contenuto del libro."—R. BONGHI in *Nuova Antologia*, Oct. 1881, pp. 717—731.

P. VERGILI MARONIS OPERA cum Prolegomenis et Commentario Critico edidit B. H. KENNEDY, S.T.P., Graecae Linguae Prof. Regius. Extra Fcap. 8vo. 5*s*.

See also Pitt Press Series, pp. 24—27.

MATHEMATICS, PHYSICAL SCIENCE, &c.

MATHEMATICAL AND PHYSICAL PAPERS. By Sir W. THOMSON, LL.D., D.C.L., F.R.S., Professor of Natural Philosophy in the University of Glasgow. Collected from different Scientific Periodicals from May 1841, to the present time. Vol. I. Demy 8vo. 18*s*. Vol. II. 15*s*. [Volume III. *In the Press*.

"Wherever exact science has found a follower Sir William Thomson's name is known as a leader and a master. For a space of 40 years each of his successive contributions to knowledge in the domain of experimental and mathematical physics has been recognized as marking a stage in the progress of the subject. But, unhappily for the mere learner, he is no writer of text-books. His eager fertility overflows into the nearest available journal . . . The papers in this volume deal largely with the subject of the dynamics of heat. They begin with two or three articles which were in part written at the age of 17, before the author had commenced residence as an undergraduate in Cambridge."—*The Times*.

"We are convinced that nothing has had a greater effect on the progress of the theories of electricity and magnetism during the last ten years than the publication of Sir W. Thomson's reprint of papers on electrostatics and magnetism, and we believe that the present volume is destined in no less degree to further the advancement of physical science."—*Glasgow Herald*.

MATHEMATICAL AND PHYSICAL PAPERS, by GEORGE GABRIEL STOKES, M.A., D.C.L., LL.D., F.R.S., Fellow of Pembroke College, and Lucasian Professor of Mathematics in the University of Cambridge. Reprinted from the Original Journals and Transactions, with Additional Notes by the Author. Vol. I. Demy 8vo. 15*s*. Vol. II. 15*s*. [Volume III. *In the Press*.

"...The same spirit pervades the papers on pure mathematics which are included in the volume. They have a severe accuracy of style which well befits the subtle nature of the subjects, and inspires the completest confidence in their author."—*The Times*.

A HISTORY OF THE THEORY OF ELASTICITY AND OF THE STRENGTH OF MATERIALS, from Galilei to the present time. VOL. I. Galilei to Saint-Venant, 1638–1850. By the late I. TODHUNTER, D. Sc., F.R.S., edited and completed by KARL PEARSON, M.A. [*Nearly ready*.

THE SCIENTIFIC PAPERS OF THE LATE PROF. J. CLERK MAXWELL. Edited by W. D. NIVEN, M.A. In 2 vols. Royal 4to. [*In the Press.*

A TREATISE ON NATURAL PHILOSOPHY. By Sir W. THOMSON, LL.D., D.C.L., F.R.S., Professor of Natural Philosophy in the University of Glasgow, and P. G. TAIT, M.A., Professor of Natural Philosophy in the University of Edinburgh. **Part I.** Demy 8vo. 16*s.* **Part II.** Demy 8vo. 18*s.*

ELEMENTS OF NATURAL PHILOSOPHY. By Professors Sir W. THOMSON and P. G. TAIT. Demy 8vo. *Second Edition.* 9*s.*

AN ATTEMPT TO TEST THE THEORIES OF CAPILLARY ACTION by FRANCIS BASHFORTH, B.D., and J. C. ADAMS, M.A., F.R.S. Demy 4to. £1. 1*s.*

A TREATISE ON THE THEORY OF DETERMINANTS and their applications in Analysis and Geometry, by R. F. SCOTT, M.A., Fellow of St John's College. Demy 8vo. 12*s.*

HYDRODYNAMICS, a Treatise on the Mathematical Theory of the Motion of Fluids, by HORACE LAMB, M.A., formerly Fellow of Trinity College, Cambridge. Demy 8vo. 12*s.*

THE ANALYTICAL THEORY OF HEAT, by JOSEPH FOURIER. Translated, with Notes, by A. FREEMAN, M.A., Fellow of St John's College, Cambridge. Demy 8vo. 16*s.*

THE ELECTRICAL RESEARCHES OF THE Hon. H. CAVENDISH, F.R.S. Written between 1771 and 1781. Edited from the original MSS. in the possession of the Duke of Devonshire, K. G., by the late J. CLERK MAXWELL, F.R.S. Demy 8vo. 18*s.*

"Every department of editorial duty appears to have been most conscientiously performed; and it must have been no small satisfaction to Prof. Maxwell to see this goodly volume completed before his life's work was done."—*Athenæum.*

AN ELEMENTARY TREATISE ON QUATERNIONS. By P. G. TAIT, M.A., Professor of Natural Philosophy in the University of Edinburgh. *Second Edition.* Demy 8vo. 14*s.*

THE MATHEMATICAL WORKS OF ISAAC BARROW, D.D. Edited by W. WHEWELL, D.D. Demy 8vo. 7*s.* 6*d.*

COUNTERPOINT. A Practical Course of Study, by Professor Sir G. A. MACFARREN, M.A., Mus. Doc. New Edition, revised. Crown 4to. 7*s.* 6*d.*

A TREATISE ON THE GENERAL PRINCIPLES OF CHEMISTRY, by M. M. PATTISON MUIR, M.A., Fellow and Prælector in Chemistry of Gonville and Caius College. Demy 8vo. 15*s.*

"The value of the book as a digest of the historical developments of chemical thought is immense."—*Academy.*

"Theoretical Chemistry has moved so rapidly of late years that most of our ordinary text books have been left far behind. German students, to be sure, possess an excellent guide to the present state of the science in 'Die Modernen Theorien der Chemie' of Prof. Lothar Meyer; but in this country the student has had to content himself with such works as Dr Tilden's 'Introduction to Chemical Philosophy', an admirable book in its way, but rather slender. Mr Pattison Muir having aimed at a more comprehensive scheme, has produced a systematic treatise on the principles of chemical philosophy which stands far in advance of any kindred work in our language. It is a treatise that requires for its due comprehension a fair acquaintance with physical science, and it can hardly be placed with advantage in the hands of any one who does not possess an extended knowledge of descriptive chemistry. But the advanced student whose mind is well equipped with an array of chemical and physical facts can turn to Mr Muir's masterly volume for unfailing help in acquiring a knowledge of the principles of modern chemistry."—*Athenæum.*

NOTES ON QUALITATIVE ANALYSIS. Concise and Explanatory. By H. J. H. FENTON, M.A., F.I.C., Demonstrator of Chemistry in the University of Cambridge. Cr. 4to. *New Edition.* 6*s.*

A TREATISE ON THE PHYSIOLOGY OF PLANTS, by S. H. VINES, M.A., Fellow of Christ's College. [*Immediately.*

A SHORT HISTORY OF GREEK MATHEMATICS. By J. GOW, Litt.D., Fellow of Trinity College. Demy 8vo. 10*s.* 6*d.*

DIOPHANTOS OF ALEXANDRIA; a Study in the History of Greek Algebra. By T. L. HEATH, B.A., Fellow of Trinity College, Cambridge. Demy 8vo. 7*s.* 6*d.*

"This study in the history of Greek Algebra is an exceedingly valuable contribution to the history of mathematics."—*Academy.*

"Der Verfasser des uns vorliegenden Werkes hat die vorhandenen Schriften Diophants einem genauen Studium unterworfen. Er hat die sämtlichen erhaltenen Aufgaben nicht ihrem Wortlaut nach übersetzt, sondern in die algebraische Zeichensprache unserer Zeit übertragen, und diese moderne Darstellung hat er auf 86 S. anhangsweise zum Abdrucke gebracht, während eine fast doppelt so starke Abhandlung vorausgeht.... Wir haben zu zeigen gesucht, dass es in dem uns vorliegenden Buche nicht an neuen Gedanken fehlt. Wir hoffen in der nicht vollständigen Uebereinstimmung, in welcher wir uns mit dem Verf. befinden, das Lob nicht erstickt zu haben, welches in jener Anerkennung liegt."—M. Cantor, *Berl. Phil. Wochenschrift.*

"The most thorough account extant of Diophantus's place, work, and critics.... [The classification of Diophantus's methods of solution taken in conjunction with the invaluable abstract, presents the English reader with a capital picture of what Greek algebraists had really accomplished.]"—*Athenæum.*

THE FOSSILS AND PALÆONTOLOGICAL AFFINITIES OF THE NEOCOMIAN DEPOSITS OF UPWARE AND BRICKHILL with Plates, being the Sedgwick Prize Essay for the Year 1879. By W. KEEPING, M.A., F.G.S. Demy 8vo. 10*s.* 6*d.*

A CATALOGUE OF BOOKS AND PAPERS ON PROTOZOA, CŒLENTERATES, WORMS, and certain smaller groups of animals, published during the years 1861—1883, by D'ARCY W. THOMPSON, B.A., Scholar of Trinity College, Cambridge. Demy 8vo. 12*s.* 6*d.*

ASTRONOMICAL OBSERVATIONS made at the Observatory of Cambridge by the late Rev. JAMES CHALLIS, M.A., F.R.S., F.R.A.S. For various Years, from 1846 to 1860.

ASTRONOMICAL OBSERVATIONS from 1861 to 1865. Vol. XXI. Royal 4to. 15*s.* From 1866 to 1869. Vol. XXII. Royal 4to. [*Nearly ready.*

A CATALOGUE OF THE COLLECTION OF BIRDS formed by the late H. E. STRICKLAND, now in the possession of the University of Cambridge. By O. SALVIN, M.A. Demy 8vo. £1. 1*s.*

A CATALOGUE OF AUSTRALIAN FOSSILS (including Tasmania and the Island of Timor), Stratigraphically and Zoologically arranged, by R. ETHERIDGE, Jun., F.G.S., Acting Palæontologist, H.M. Geol. Survey of Scotland. Demy 8vo. 10*s.* 6*d.*

ILLUSTRATIONS OF COMPARATIVE ANATOMY, VERTEBRATE AND INVERTEBRATE, for the Use of Students in the Museum of Zoology and Comparative Anatomy. Second Edition. Demy 8vo. 2*s.* 6*d.*

A SYNOPSIS OF THE CLASSIFICATION OF THE BRITISH PALÆOZOIC ROCKS, by the Rev. ADAM SEDGWICK, M.A., F.R.S., and FREDERICK M'COY, F.G.S. One vol., Royal 4to. Plates, £1. 1*s.*

A CATALOGUE OF THE COLLECTION OF CAMBRIAN AND SILURIAN FOSSILS contained in the Geological Museum of the University of Cambridge, by J. W. SALTER, F.G.S. With a Portrait of PROFESSOR SEDGWICK. Royal 4to. 7*s.* 6*d.*

CATALOGUE OF OSTEOLOGICAL SPECIMENS contained in the Anatomical Museum of the University of Cambridge. Demy 8vo. 2*s.* 6*d.*

LAW.

A SELECTION OF CASES ON THE ENGLISH LAW OF CONTRACT.

By GERARD BROWN FINCH, M.A., of Lincoln's Inn, Barrister at Law; Law Lecturer and late Fellow of Queens' College, Cambridge. Royal 8vo. 28*s.*

"An invaluable guide towards the best method of legal study."—*Law Quarterly Review.*

THE INFLUENCE OF THE ROMAN LAW ON THE LAW OF ENGLAND.

Being the Yorke Prize Essay for 1884. By T. E. SCRUTTON, M.A. Demy 8vo. 10*s.* 6*d.*

"Legal work of just the kind that a learned University should promote by its prizes."—*Law Quarterly Review.*

AN ANALYSIS OF CRIMINAL LIABILITY.

By E. C. CLARK, LL.D., Regius Professor of Civil Law in the University of Cambridge, also of Lincoln's Inn, Barrister-at-Law. Crown 8vo. 7*s.* 6*d.*

"Prof. Clark's little book is the substance of lectures delivered by him upon those portions of Austin's work on jurisprudence which deal with the "operation of sanctions" . . . Students of jurisprudence will find much to interest and instruct them in the work of Prof. Clark."—*Athenæum.*

PRACTICAL JURISPRUDENCE, a Comment on AUSTIN.

By E. C. CLARK, LL.D. Regius Professor of Civil Law. Crown 8vo. 9*s.*

"Damit schliesst dieses inhaltreiche und nach allen Seiten anregende Buch über Practical Jurisprudence."—König. *Centralblatt für Rechtswissenschaft.*

A SELECTION OF THE STATE TRIALS.

By J. W. WILLIS-BUND, M.A., LL.B., Barrister-at-Law, Professor of Constitutional Law and History, University College, London. Crown 8vo. Vols. I. and II. In 3 parts. **Now reduced to 30*s.*** (*originally published at* 46*s.*)

"This work is a very useful contribution to that important branch of the constitutional history of England which is concerned with the growth and development of the law of treason, as it may be gathered from trials before the ordinary courts. The author has very wisely distinguished these cases from those of impeachment for treason before Parliament, which he proposes to treat in a future volume under the general head 'Proceedings in Parliament.'"—*The Academy.*

"This is a work of such obvious utility that the only wonder is that no one should have undertaken it before . . . In many respects therefore, although the trials are more or less abridged, this is for the ordinary student's purpose not only a more handy, but a more useful work than Howell's."—*Saturday Review.*

"But, although the book is most interesting to the historian of constitutional law, it is also not without considerable value to those who seek information with regard to procedure and the growth of the law of evidence. We should add that Mr Willis-Bund has given short prefaces and appendices to the trials, so as to form a connected narrative of the events in history to which they relate. We can thoroughly recommend the book."—*Law Times.*

"To a large class of readers Mr Willis-Bund's compilation will thus be of great assistance, for he presents in a convenient form a judicious selection of the principal statutes and the leading cases bearing on the crime of treason . . . For all classes of readers these volumes possess an indirect interest, arising from the nature of the cases themselves, from the men who were actors in them, and from the numerous points of social life which are incidentally illustrated in the course of the trials."—*Athenæum.*

THE FRAGMENTS OF THE PERPETUAL EDICT OF SALVIUS JULIANUS,

collected, arranged, and annotated by BRYAN WALKER, M.A., LL.D., Law Lecturer of St John's College, and late Fellow of Corpus Christi College, Cambridge. Crown 8vo. 6*s.*

"In the present book we have the fruits of the same kind of thorough and well-ordered study which was brought to bear upon the notes to the Commentaries and the Institutes . . . Hitherto the Edict has been almost inaccessible to the ordinary English student, and such a student will be interested as well as perhaps surprised to find how abundantly the extant fragments illustrate and clear up points which have attracted his attention in the Commentaries, or the Institutes, or the Digest."—*Law Times.*

AN INTRODUCTION TO THE STUDY OF JUSTINIAN'S DIGEST. Containing an account of its composition and of the Jurists used or referred to therein, together with a full Commentary on one Title (de usufructu), by HENRY JOHN ROBY, M.A., formerly Prof. of Jurisprudence, University College, London. Demy 8vo. 18*s.*

"Not an obscurity, philological, historical, or legal, has been left unsifted. More informing aid still has been supplied to the student of the Digest at large by a preliminary account, covering nearly 300 pages, of the mode of composition of the Digest, and of the jurists whose decisions and arguments constitute its substance. Nowhere else can a clearer view be obtained of the personal succession by which the tradition of Roman legal science was sustained and developed. Roman law, almost more than Roman legions, was the backbone of the Roman commonwealth. Mr Roby, by his careful sketch of the sages of Roman law, from Sextus Papirius, under Tarquin the Proud, to the Byzantine Bar, has contributed to render the tenacity and durability of the most enduring polity the world has ever experienced somewhat more intelligible."—*The Times.*

THE COMMENTARIES OF GAIUS AND RULES OF ULPIAN. With a Translation and Notes, by J. T. ABDY, LL.D., Judge of County Courts, late Regius Professor of Laws in the University of Cambridge, and BRYAN WALKER, M.A., LL.D., Law Lecturer of St John's College, Cambridge, formerly Law Student of Trinity Hall and Chancellor's Medallist for Legal Studies. New Edition by BRYAN WALKER. Crown 8vo. 16*s.*

"As scholars and as editors Messrs Abdy and Walker have done their work well . . . For one thing the editors deserve special commendation. They have presented Gaius to the reader with few notes and those merely by way of reference or necessary explanation. Thus the Roman jurist is allowed to speak for himself, and the reader feels that he is really studying Roman law in the original, and not a fanciful representation of it."—*Athenæum.*

THE INSTITUTES OF JUSTINIAN, translated with Notes by J. T. ABDY, LL.D., and BRYAN WALKER, M.A., LL.D. Crown 8vo. 16*s.*

"We welcome here a valuable contribution to the study of jurisprudence. The text of the *Institutes* is occasionally perplexing, even to practised scholars, whose knowledge of classical models does not always avail them in dealing with the technicalities of legal phraseology. Nor can the ordinary dictionaries be expected to furnish all the help that is wanted. This translation will then be of great use. To the ordinary student, whose attention is distracted from the subject-matter by the difficulty of struggling through the language in which it is contained, it will be almost indispensable."—*Spectator.*

"The notes are learned and carefully compiled, and this edition will be found useful to students."—*Law Times.*

SELECTED TITLES FROM THE DIGEST, annotated by B. WALKER, M.A., LL.D. Part I. Mandati vel Contra. Digest XVII. I. Crown 8vo. 5*s.*

"This small volume is published as an experiment. The author proposes to publish an annotated edition and translation of several books of the Digest if this one is received with favour. We are pleased to be able to say that Mr Walker deserves credit for the way in which he has performed the task undertaken. The translation, as might be expected, is scholarly." —*Law Times.*

—— Part II. De Adquirendo rerum dominio and De Adquirenda vel amittenda possessione. Digest XLI. I and II. Crown 8vo. 6*s.*

—— Part III. De Condictionibus. Digest XII. I and 4—7 and Digest XIII. I—3. Crown 8vo. 6*s.*

GROTIUS DE JURE BELLI ET PACIS, with the Notes of Barbeyrac and others; accompanied by an abridged Translation of the Text, by W. WHEWELL, D.D. late Master of Trinity College. 3 Vols. Demy 8vo. 12*s.* The translation separate, 6*s.*

HISTORY.

LIFE AND TIMES OF STEIN, OR GERMANY AND PRUSSIA IN THE NAPOLEONIC AGE, by J. R. SEELEY, M.A., Regius Professor of Modern History in the University of Cambridge, with Portraits and Maps. 3 Vols. Demy 8vo. **Now reduced to 30s.** (*originally published at 48s.*)

"DR BUSCH'S volume has made people think and talk even more than usual of Prince Bismarck, and Professor Seeley's very learned work on Stein will turn attention to an earlier and an almost equally eminent German statesman. It has been the good fortune of Prince Bismarck to help to raise Prussia to a position which she had never before attained, and to complete the work of German unification. The frustrated labours of Stein in the same field were also very great, and well worthy to be taken into account. He was one, perhaps the chief, of the illustrious group of strangers who came to the rescue of Prussia in her darkest hour, about the time of the inglorious Peace of Tilsit, and who laboured to put life and order into her dispirited army, her impoverished finances, and her inefficient Civil Service. Stein strove, too, —no man more,—for the cause of unification when it seemed almost folly to hope for success. Englishmen will feel very pardonable pride at seeing one of their countrymen undertake to write the history of a period from the investigation of which even laborious Germans are apt to shrink."—*Times*.

"In a notice of this kind scant justice can be done to a work like the one before us; no short *résumé* can give even the most meagre notion of the contents of these volumes, which contain no page that is superfluous, and none that is uninteresting .... To understand the Germany of to-day one must study the Germany of many yesterdays, and now that study has been made easy by this work, to which no one can hesitate to assign a very high place among those recent histories which have aimed at original research."—*Athenæum*.

"We congratulate Cambridge and her Professor of History on the appearance of such a noteworthy production. And we may add that it is something upon which we may congratulate England that on the especial field of the Germans, history, on the history of their own country, by the use of their own literary weapons, an Englishman has produced a history of Germany in the Napoleonic age far superior to any that exists in German."—*Examiner*.

THE DESPATCHES OF EARL GOWER, English Ambassador at the court of Versailles from June 1790 to August 1792, to which are added the Despatches of Mr Lindsay and Mr Munro, and the Diary of Lord Palmerston in France during July and August 1791. By OSCAR BROWNING, M.A., Fellow of King's College, Cambridge. Demy 8vo. 15s.

THE GROWTH OF ENGLISH INDUSTRY AND COMMERCE. By W. CUNNINGHAM, B.D., late Deputy to the Knightbridge Professor in the University of Cambridge. With Maps and Charts. Crown 8vo. 12s.

"Mr Cunningham is not likely to disappoint any readers except such as begin by mistaking the character of his book. He does not promise, and does not give, an account of the dimensions to which English industry and commerce have grown. It is with the process of growth that he is concerned; and this process he traces with the philosophical insight which distinguishes between what is important and what is trivial."—*Guardian*.

CHRONOLOGICAL TABLES OF GREEK HISTORY. Accompanied by a short narrative of events, with references to the sources of information and extracts from the ancient authorities, by CARL PETER. Translated from the German by G. CHAWNER, M.A., Fellow of King's College, Cambridge. Demy 4to. 10s.

"As a handy book of reference for genuine students, or even for learned men who want to lay their hands on an authority for some particular point as quickly as possible, the *Tables* are useful."—*Academy*.

CHRONOLOGICAL TABLES OF ROMAN HISTORY. By the same. [*Preparing*.

KINSHIP AND MARRIAGE IN EARLY ARABIA, by W. ROBERTSON SMITH, M.A., LL.D., Lord Almoner's Professor of Arabic in the University of Cambridge. Crown 8vo. 7s. 6d.

"It is clearly and vividly written, full of curious and picturesque material, and incidentally throws light, not merely on the social history of Arabia, but on the earlier passages of Old Testament history.... We must be grateful to him for so valuable a contribution to the early history of social organisation."—*Scotsman*.

TRAVELS IN NORTHERN ARABIA IN 1876 AND 1877. By CHARLES M. DOUGHTY, of Gonville and Caius College. With Illustrations. Demy 8vo. [*In the Press.*

HISTORY OF NEPĀL, translated by MUNSHĪ SHEW SHUNKER SINGH and PANDIT SHRĪ GUNĀNAND; edited with an Introductory Sketch of the Country and People by Dr D. WRIGHT, late Residency Surgeon at Kāṭhmāṇḍū, and with facsimiles of native drawings, and portraits of Sir JUNG BAHĀDUR, the KING OF NEPĀL, &c. Super-royal 8vo. **Now reduced to 10*s.* 6*d.*** (*published at 21s.*)

"The Cambridge University Press have done well in publishing this work. Such translations are valuable not only to the historian but also to the ethnologist; . . . Dr Wright's Introduction is based on personal inquiry and observation, is written intelligently and candidly, and adds much to the value of the volume"—*Nature.*

A JOURNAL OF LITERARY AND ARCHÆOLOGICAL RESEARCH IN NEPAL AND NORTHERN INDIA, during the Winter of 1884–5. By CECIL BENDALL, M.A., Fellow of Gonville and Caius College, Cambridge; Professor of Sanskrit in University College, London. Demy 8vo.

THE UNIVERSITY OF CAMBRIDGE FROM THE EARLIEST TIMES TO THE ROYAL INJUNCTIONS OF 1535, by J. B. MULLINGER, M.A., Lecturer on History and Librarian to St John's College. Part I. Demy 8vo. (734 pp.), 12*s.*

Part II. From the Royal Injunctions of 1535 to the Accession of Charles the First. Demy 8vo. 18*s.*

"That Mr Mullinger's work should admit of being regarded as a continuous narrative, in which character it has no predecessors worth mentioning, is one of the many advantages it possesses over annalistic compilations, even so valuable as Cooper's, as well as over *Athenae.*"—Prof. A. W. Ward in the *Academy.*

"Mr Mullinger's narrative omits nothing which is required by the fullest interpretation of his subject. He shews in the statutes of the Colleges, the internal organization of the University, its connection with national problems, its studies, its social life, and the activity of its leading members. All this he combines in a form which is eminently readable."—PROF. CREIGHTON in *Cont. Review.*

"Mr Mullinger has succeeded perfectly in presenting the earnest and thoughtful student with a thorough and trustworthy history."—*Guardian.*

"The entire work is a model of accurate and industrious scholarship. The same qualities that distinguished the earlier volume are again visible, and the whole is still conspicuous for minuteness and fidelity of workmanship and breadth and toleration of view."—*Notes and Queries.*

"Mr Mullinger displays an admirable thoroughness in his work. Nothing could be more exhaustive and conscientious than his method: and his style...is picturesque and elevated."—*Times.*

HISTORY OF THE COLLEGE OF ST JOHN THE EVANGELIST, by THOMAS BAKER, B.D., Ejected Fellow. Edited by JOHN E. B. MAYOR, M.A. Two Vols. Demy 8vo. 24*s.*

"To antiquaries the book will be a source of almost inexhaustible amusement, by historians it will be found a work of considerable service on questions respecting our social progress in past times; and the care and thoroughness with which Mr Mayor has discharged his editorial functions are creditable to his learning and industry."—*Athenæum.*

"The work displays very wide reading, and it will be of great use to members of the college and of the university, and, perhaps, of still greater use to students of English history, ecclesiastical, political, social, literary and academical, who have hitherto had to be content with 'Dyer.'"—*Academy.*

SCHOLAE ACADEMICAE: some Account of the Studies at the English Universities in the Eighteenth Century. By CHRISTOPHER WORDSWORTH, M.A., Fellow of Peterhouse. Demy 8vo. **Now reduced to 10*s.* 6*d.*** (*originally published at 15s.*)

"Mr Wordsworth has collected a great quantity of minute and curious information about the working of Cambridge institutions in the last century, with an occasional comparison of the corresponding state of things at Oxford. . . . To a great extent it is purely a book of reference, and as such it will be of permanent value for the historical knowledge of English education and learning."—*Saturday Review.*

"Of the whole volume it may be said that it is a genuine service rendered to the study of University history, and that the habits of thought of any writer educated at either seat of learning in the last century will, in many cases, be far better understood after a consideration of the materials here collected."—*Academy.*

THE ARCHITECTURAL HISTORY OF THE UNIVERSITY OF CAMBRIDGE AND OF THE COLLEGES OF CAMBRIDGE AND ETON, by the late ROBERT WILLIS, M.A. F.R.S., Jacksonian Professor in the University of Cambridge. Edited with large Additions and a Continuation to the present time by JOHN WILLIS CLARK, M.A., formerly Fellow of Trinity College, Cambridge. Four Vols. Super Royal 8vo. £6. 6*s*.

Also a limited Edition of the same, consisting of 120 numbered Copies only, large paper Quarto; the woodcuts and steel engravings mounted on India paper; of which 100 copies are now offered for sale, at Twenty-five Guineas **net** each set.

MISCELLANEOUS.

A CATALOGUE OF ANCIENT MARBLES IN GREAT BRITAIN, by Prof. ADOLF MICHAELIS. Translated by C. A. M. FENNELL, Litt. D., late Fellow of Jesus College. Royal 8vo. Roxburgh (Morocco back), £2. 2*s*.

"The object of the present work of Michaelis is to describe and make known the vast treasures of ancient sculpture now accumulated in the galleries of Great Britain, the extent and value of which are scarcely appreciated, and chiefly so because there has hitherto been little accessible information about them. To the loving labours of a learned German the owners of art treasures in England are for the second time indebted for a full description of their rich possessions. Waagen gave to the private collections of pictures the advantage of his inspection and cultivated acquaintance with art, and now Michaelis performs the same office for the still less known private hoards of antique sculptures for which our country is so remarkable. The book is beautifully executed, and with its few handsome plates, and excellent indexes, does much credit to the Cambridge Press. It has not been printed in German, but appears for the first time in the English translation. All lovers of true art and of good work should be grateful to the Syndics of the University Press for the liberal facilities afforded by them towards the production of this important volume by Professor Michaelis." —*Saturday Review.*

"Professor Michaelis has achieved so high a fame as an authority in classical archæology that it seems unnecessary to say how good a book this is."—*The Antiquary.*

RHODES IN ANCIENT TIMES. By CECIL TORR, M.A. With six plates. 10*s*. 6*d*.

THE WOODCUTTERS OF THE NETHERLANDS during the last quarter of the Fifteenth Century. In three parts. I. History of the Woodcutters. II. Catalogue of their Woodcuts. III. List of the Books containing Woodcuts. By WILLIAM MARTIN CONWAY. Demy 8vo. 10*s*. 6*d*.

A GRAMMAR OF THE IRISH LANGUAGE. By Prof. WINDISCH. Translated by Dr NORMAN MOORE. Crown 8vo. 7*s*. 6*d*.

LECTURES ON TEACHING, delivered in the University of Cambridge in the Lent Term, 1880. By J. G. FITCH, M.A., LL.D. Her Majesty's Inspector of Training Colleges. Cr. 8vo. New Edit. 5*s*.

"As principal of a training college and as a Government inspector of schools, Mr Fitch has got at his fingers' ends the working of primary education, while as assistant commissioner to the late Endowed Schools Commission he has seen something of the machinery of our higher schools . . . Mr Fitch's book covers so wide a field and touches on so many burning questions that we must be content to recommend it as the best existing *vade mecum* for the teacher." —*Pall Mall Gazette.*

"Therefore, without reviewing the book for the second time, we are glad to avail ourselves of the opportunity of calling attention to the re-issue of the volume in the five-shilling form, bringing it within the reach of the rank and file of the profession. We cannot let the occasion pass without making special reference to the excellent section on 'punishments' in the lecture on 'Discipline.'"—*School Board Chronicle.*

For other books on Education, see Pitt Press Series, pp. 30, 31.

"FROM SHAKESPEARE TO POPE": an Inquiry into the causes and phenomena of the rise of Classical Poetry in England. By EDMUND GOSSE, M.A., Clark Lecturer in English Literature at Trinity College, Cambridge. Crown 8vo. 6*s.*

THE LITERATURE OF THE FRENCH RENAISSANCE. An Introductory Essay. By A. A. TILLEY, M.A., Fellow and Tutor of King's College, Cambridge. Crown 8vo. 6*s.*

STUDIES IN THE LITERARY RELATIONS OF ENGLAND WITH GERMANY IN THE SIXTEENTH CENTURY. By C. H. HERFORD, M.A. [*In the Press.*

CATALOGUE OF THE HEBREW MANUSCRIPTS preserved in the University Library, Cambridge. By Dr S. M. SCHILLER-SZINESSY. Volume I. containing Section I. *The Holy Scriptures;* Section II. *Commentaries on the Bible.* Demy 8vo. 9*s.*
Volume II. *In the Press.*

A CATALOGUE OF THE MANUSCRIPTS preserved in the Library of the University of Cambridge. Demy 8vo. 5 Vols. 10*s.* each. INDEX TO THE CATALOGUE. Demy 8vo. 10*s.*

A CATALOGUE OF ADVERSARIA and printed books containing MS. notes, preserved in the Library of the University of Cambridge. 3*s.* 6*d.*

THE ILLUMINATED MANUSCRIPTS IN THE LIBRARY OF THE FITZWILLIAM MUSEUM, Catalogued with Descriptions, and an Introduction, by W. G. SEARLE, M.A., late Fellow of Queens' College, Cambridge Demy 8vo. 7*s.* 6*d*

A CHRONOLOGICAL LIST OF THE GRACES, Documents, and other Papers in the University Registry which concern the University Library. Demy 8vo. 2*s.* 6*d.*

CATALOGUS BIBLIOTHECÆ BURCKHARDTIANÆ. Demy 4to. 5*s.*

GRADUATI CANTABRIGIENSES: SIVE CATALOGUS exhibens nomina eorum quos ab Anno Academico Admissionum MDCCC usque ad octavum diem Octobris MDCCCLXXXIV gradu quocunque ornavit Academia Cantabrigiensis, e libris subscriptionum desumptus. Cura HENRICI RICHARDS LUARD S. T. P. Coll. SS. Trin. Socii atque Academiæ Registrarii. Demy 8vo. 12*s.* 6*d.*

STATUTES OF THE UNIVERSITY OF CAMBRIDGE and for the Colleges therein, made published and approved (1878—1882) under the Universities of Oxford and Cambridge Act, 1877. With an Appendix. Demy 8vo. 16*s.*

STATUTES OF THE UNIVERSITY OF CAMBRIDGE. With some Acts of Parliament relating to the University. Demy 8vo. 3*s.* 6*d.*

ORDINANCES OF THE UNIVERSITY OF CAMBRIDGE. Demy 8vo., cloth. 7*s.* 6*d.*

TRUSTS, STATUTES AND DIRECTIONS affecting (1) The Professorships of the University. (2) The Scholarships and Prizes. (3) Other Gifts and Endowments. Demy 8vo. 5*s.*

COMPENDIUM OF UNIVERSITY REGULATIONS, for the use of persons in Statu Pupillari. Demy 8vo. 6*d.*

The Cambridge Bible for Schools and Colleges.

GENERAL EDITOR: THE VERY REVEREND J. J. S. PEROWNE, D.D., DEAN OF PETERBOROUGH.

"It is difficult to commend too highly this excellent series, the volumes of which are now becoming numerous."—*Guardian.*

"The modesty of the general title of this series has, we believe, led many to misunderstand its character and underrate its value. The books are well suited for study in the upper forms of our best schools, but not the less are they adapted to the wants of all Bible students who are not specialists. We doubt, indeed, whether any of the numerous popular commentaries recently issued in this country will be found more serviceable for general use."—*Academy.*

"Of great value. The whole series of comments for schools is highly esteemed by students capable of forming a judgment. The books are scholarly without being pretentious: information is so given as to be easily understood."—*Sword and Trowel.*

The Very Reverend J. J. S. PEROWNE, D.D., Dean of Peterborough, has undertaken the general editorial supervision of the work, assisted by a staff of eminent coadjutors. Some of the books have been already edited or undertaken by the following gentlemen:

Rev. A. CARR, M.A., *late Assistant Master at Wellington College.*
Rev. T. K. CHEYNE, M.A., D.D., *late Fellow of Balliol College, Oxford.*
Rev. S. COX, *Nottingham.*
Rev. A. B. DAVIDSON, D.D., *Professor of Hebrew, Edinburgh.*
The Ven. F. W. FARRAR, D.D., *Archdeacon of Westminster.*
Rev. C. D. GINSBURG, LL.D.
Rev. A. E. HUMPHREYS, M.A., *late Fellow of Trinity College, Cambridge.*
Rev. A. F. KIRKPATRICK, M.A., *Fellow of Trinity College, Regius Professor of Hebrew.*
Rev. J. J. LIAS, M.A., *late Professor at St David's College, Lampeter.*
Rev. J. R. LUMBY, D.D., *Norrisian Professor of Divinity.*
Rev. G. F. MACLEAR, D.D., *Warden of St Augustine's College, Canterbury.*
Rev. H. C. G. MOULE, M.A., *late Fellow of Trinity College, Principal of Ridley Hall, Cambridge.*
Rev. W. F. MOULTON, D.D., *Head Master of the Leys School, Cambridge.*
Rev. E. H. PEROWNE, D.D., *Master of Corpus Christi College, Cambridge.*
The Ven. T. T. PEROWNE, M.A., *Archdeacon of Norwich.*
Rev. A. PLUMMER, M.A., D.D., *Master of University College, Durham.*
The Very Rev. E. H. PLUMPTRE, D.D., *Dean of Wells.*
Rev. W. SIMCOX, M.A., *Rector of Weyhill, Hants.*
The Very Rev. R. PAYNE SMITH, D.D., *Dean of Canterbury.*
W. ROBERTSON SMITH, M.A., *Lord Almoner's Professor of Arabic.*
Rev. H. D. M. SPENCE, M.A., *Hon. Canon of Gloucester Cathedral.*
Rev. A. W. STREANE, M.A., *Fellow of Corpus Christi College, Cambridge.*

London: C. J. CLAY & SON, Cambridge University Press Warehouse, Ave Maria Lane.

THE CAMBRIDGE BIBLE FOR SCHOOLS & COLLEGES.

Continued.

Now Ready. Cloth, Extra Fcap. 8vo.

THE BOOK OF JOSHUA. By the Rev. G. F. MACLEAR, D.D. With 2 Maps. 2*s.* 6*d.*

THE BOOK OF JUDGES. By the Rev. J. J. LIAS, M.A. With Map. 3*s.* 6*d.*

THE FIRST BOOK OF SAMUEL. By the Rev. Professor KIRKPATRICK, M.A. With Map. 3*s.* 6*d.*

THE SECOND BOOK OF SAMUEL. By the Rev. Professor KIRKPATRICK, M.A. With 2 Maps. 3*s.* 6*d.*

THE BOOK OF JOB. By the Rev. A. B. DAVIDSON, D.D. 5*s.*

THE BOOK OF ECCLESIASTES. By the Very Rev. E. H. PLUMPTRE, D.D., Dean of Wells. 5*s.*

THE BOOK OF JEREMIAH. By the Rev. A. W. STREANE, M.A. With Map. 4*s.* 6*d.*

THE BOOK OF HOSEA. By Rev. T. K. CHEYNE, M.A., D.D. 3*s.*

THE BOOKS OF OBADIAH AND JONAH. By Archdeacon PEROWNE. 2*s.* 6*d.*

THE BOOK OF MICAH. By Rev. T. K. CHEYNE, M.A., D.D. 1*s.* 6*d.*

THE BOOKS OF HAGGAI AND ZECHARIAH. By Archdeacon PEROWNE. 3*s.*

THE GOSPEL ACCORDING TO ST MATTHEW. By the Rev. A. CARR, M.A. With 2 Maps. 2*s.* 6*d.*

THE GOSPEL ACCORDING TO ST MARK. By the Rev. G. F. MACLEAR, D.D. With 4 Maps. 2*s.* 6*d.*

THE GOSPEL ACCORDING TO ST LUKE. By Archdeacon F. W. FARRAR. With 4 Maps. 4*s.* 6*d.*

THE GOSPEL ACCORDING TO ST JOHN. By the Rev. A. PLUMMER, M.A., D.D. With 4 Maps. 4*s.* 6*d.*

THE ACTS OF THE APOSTLES. By the Rev. Professor LUMBY, D.D. With 4 Maps. 4*s.* 6*d.*

THE EPISTLE TO THE ROMANS. By the Rev. H. C. G. MOULE, M.A. 3*s.* 6*d.*

THE FIRST EPISTLE TO THE CORINTHIANS. By the Rev. J. J. LIAS, M.A. With a Map and Plan. 2*s.*

THE SECOND EPISTLE TO THE CORINTHIANS. By the Rev. J. J. LIAS, M.A. 2*s.*

THE EPISTLE TO THE HEBREWS. By Archdeacon FARRAR. 3*s.* 6*d.*

THE GENERAL EPISTLE OF ST JAMES. By the Very Rev. E. H. PLUMPTRE, D.D., Dean of Wells. 1*s.* 6*d.*

THE EPISTLES OF ST PETER AND ST JUDE. By the same Editor. 2*s.* 6*d.*

THE EPISTLES OF ST JOHN. By the Rev. A. PLUMMER, M.A., D.D. 3*s.* 6*d.*

THE CAMBRIDGE BIBLE FOR SCHOOLS & COLLEGES.

Continued.

Preparing.

THE BOOK OF GENESIS. By the Very Rev. R. PAYNE SMITH, D.D.

THE BOOKS OF EXODUS, NUMBERS AND DEUTERONOMY. By the Rev. C. D. GINSBURG, LL.D.

THE FIRST AND SECOND BOOKS OF KINGS. By the Rev. Prof. LUMBY, D.D.

THE BOOK OF PSALMS. By the Rev. Prof. KIRKPATRICK, M.A.

THE BOOK OF ISAIAH. By Prof. W. ROBERTSON SMITH, M.A.

THE BOOK OF EZEKIEL. By the Rev. A. B. DAVIDSON, D.D.

THE EPISTLE TO THE GALATIANS. By the Rev. E. H. PEROWNE, D.D.

THE EPISTLES TO THE EPHESIANS, PHILIPPIANS, COLOSSIANS AND PHILEMON. By the Rev. H. C. G. MOULE, M.A.

THE BOOK OF REVELATION. By the Rev. W. SIMCOX, M.A.

THE CAMBRIDGE GREEK TESTAMENT

FOR SCHOOLS AND COLLEGES,

with a Revised Text, based on the most recent critical authorities, and English Notes, prepared under the direction of the General Editor,

THE VERY REVEREND J. J. S. PEROWNE, D.D.

Now Ready.

THE GOSPEL ACCORDING TO ST MATTHEW. By the Rev. A. CARR, M.A. With 4 Maps. 4*s*. 6*d*.

"Copious illustrations, gathered from a great variety of sources, make his notes a very valuable aid to the student. They are indeed remarkably interesting, while all explanations on meanings, applications, and the like are distinguished by their lucidity and good sense."—*Pall Mall Gazette.*

THE GOSPEL ACCORDING TO ST MARK. By the Rev. G. F. MACLEAR, D.D. With 3 Maps. 4*s*. 6*d*.

"The Cambridge Greek Testament, of which Dr Maclear's edition of the Gospel according to St Mark is a volume, certainly supplies a want. Without pretending to compete with the leading commentaries, or to embody very much original research, it forms a most satisfactory introduction to the study of the New Testament in the original . . . Dr Maclear's introduction contains all that is known of St Mark's life, with references to passages in the New Testament in which he is mentioned; an account of the circumstances in which the Gospel was composed, with an estimate of the influence of St Peter's teaching upon St Mark; an excellent sketch of the special characteristics of this Gospel; an analysis, and a chapter on the text of the New Testament generally . . . The work is completed by three good maps."—*Saturday Review.*

THE GOSPEL ACCORDING TO ST LUKE. By Archdeacon FARRAR. With 4 Maps. 6*s*.

THE GOSPEL ACCORDING TO ST JOHN. By the Rev. A. PLUMMER, M.A., D.D. With 4 Maps. 6*s*.

"A valuable addition has also been made to 'The Cambridge Greek Testament for Schools,' Dr Plummer's notes on 'the Gospel according to St John' are scholarly, concise, and instructive, and embody the results of much thought and wide reading."—*Expositor.*

THE ACTS OF THE APOSTLES. By the Rev. Prof. LUMBY, D.D., with 4 Maps. 6*s*.

THE FIRST EPISTLE TO THE CORINTHIANS. By the Rev. J. J. LIAS, M.A. [*Nearly ready.*

THE EPISTLE TO THE HEBREWS. By Archdeacon FARRAR. [*In the Press.*

THE EPISTLES OF ST JOHN. By the Rev. A. PLUMMER, M.A., D.D. 4*s*.

THE PITT PRESS SERIES.

I. GREEK.

SOPHOCLES.—OEDIPUS TYRANNUS. School Edition, with Introduction and Commentary, by R. C. JEBB, Litt. D., LL.D., Professor of Greek in the University of Glasgow. *4s. 6d.*

THE ANABASIS OF XENOPHON, BOOKS I. III. IV. and V. With a Map and English Notes by ALFRED PRETOR, M.A., Fellow of St Catharine's College, Cambridge. *2s.* each.

"In Mr Pretor's edition of the Anabasis the text of Kühner has been followed in the main, while the exhaustive and admirable notes of the great German editor have been largely utilised. These notes deal with the minutest as well as the most important difficulties in construction, and all questions of history, antiquity, and geography are briefly but very effectually elucidated."—*The Examiner.*

"We welcome this addition to the other books of the *Anabasis* so ably edited by Mr Pretor. Although originally intended for the use of candidates at the university local examinations, yet this edition will be found adapted not only to meet the wants of the junior student, but even advanced scholars will find much in this work that will repay its perusal."—*The Schoolmaster.*

"Mr Pretor's 'Anabasis of Xenophon, Book IV.' displays a union of accurate Cambridge scholarship, with experience of what is required by learners gained in examining middle-class schools. The text is large and clearly printed, and the notes explain all difficulties. . . . Mr Pretor's notes seem to be all that could be wished as regards grammar, geography, and other matters."—*The Academy.*

BOOKS II. VI. and VII. By the same Editor. *2s. 6d.* each.

"Another Greek text, designed it would seem for students preparing for the local examinations, is 'Xenophon's Anabasis,' Book II., with English Notes, by Alfred Pretor, M.A. The editor has exercised his usual discrimination in utilising the text and notes of Kuhner, with the occasional assistance of the best hints of Schneider, Vollbrecht and Macmichael on critical matters, and of Mr R. W. Taylor on points of history and geography. . . When Mr Pretor commits himself to Commentator's work, he is eminently helpful. . . Had we to introduce a young Greek scholar to Xenophon, we should esteem ourselves fortunate in having Pretor's text-book as our chart and guide."—*Contemporary Review.*

THE ANABASIS OF XENOPHON, by A. PRETOR, M.A., Text and Notes, complete in two Volumes. *7s. 6d.*

AGESILAUS OF XENOPHON. The Text revised with Critical and Explanatory Notes, Introduction, Analysis, and Indices. By H. HAILSTONE, M.A., late Scholar of Peterhouse. *2s. 6d.*

ARISTOPHANES—RANAE. With English Notes and Introduction by W. C. GREEN, M.A., late Assistant Master at Rugby School. *3s. 6d.*

ARISTOPHANES—AVES. By the same Editor. *New Edition. 3s. 6d.*

"The notes to both plays are excellent. Much has been done in these two volumes to render the study of Aristophanes a real treat to a boy instead of a drudgery, by helping him to understand the fun and to express it in his mother tongue."—*The Examiner.*

ARISTOPHANES—PLUTUS. By the same Editor. *3s. 6d.*

EURIPIDES. HERCULES FURENS. With Introductions, Notes and Analysis. By A. GRAY, M.A., Fellow of Jesus College, and J. T. HUTCHINSON, M.A., Christ's College. New Edition, with additions. *2s.*

"Messrs Hutchinson and Gray have produced a careful and useful edition."—*Saturday Review.*

EURIPIDES HERACLEIDÆ. With Introduction and Critical Notes by E. A. BECK, M.A., Fellow of Trinity Hall. *3s. 6d.*

LUCIANI SOMNIUM CHARON PISCATOR ET DE LUCTU, with English Notes by W. E. HEITLAND, M.A., Fellow of St John's College, Cambridge. New Edition, with Appendix. 3*s*. 6*d*.

OUTLINES OF THE PHILOSOPHY OF ARISTOTLE. Edited by E. WALLACE, M.A. (See p. 31.)

II. LATIN.

M. T. CICERONIS DE AMICITIA. Edited by J. S. REID, Litt. D., Fellow and Tutor of Gonville and Caius College. New Edition, with Additions. 3*s*. 6*d*.

"Mr Reid has decidedly attained his aim, namely, 'a thorough examination of the Latinity of the dialogue.'..... The revision of the text is most valuable, and comprehends sundry acute corrections.... This volume, like Mr Reid's other editions, is a solid gain to the scholarship of the country."—*Athenæum*.

"A more distinct gain to scholarship is Mr Reid's able and thorough edition of the *De Amicitiâ* of Cicero, a work of which, whether we regard the exhaustive introduction or the instructive and most suggestive commentary, it would be difficult to speak too highly. . . . When we come to the commentary, we are only amazed by its fulness in proportion to its bulk. Nothing is overlooked which can tend to enlarge the learner's general knowledge of Ciceronian Latin or to elucidate the text."—*Saturday Review*.

M. T. CICERONIS CATO MAJOR DE SENECTUTE. Edited by J. S. REID, Litt. D. 3*s*. 6*d*.

"The notes are excellent and scholarlike, adapted for the upper forms of public schools, and likely to be useful even to more advanced students."—*Guardian*.

M. T. CICERONIS ORATIO PRO ARCHIA POETA. Edited by J. S. REID, Litt. D. Revised Edition. 2*s*.

"It is an admirable specimen of careful editing. An Introduction tells us everything we could wish to know about Archias, about Cicero's connexion with him, about the merits of the trial, and the genuineness of the speech. The text is well and carefully printed. The notes are clear and scholar-like.... No boy can master this little volume without feeling that he has advanced a long step in scholarship."—*The Academy*.

M. T. CICERONIS PRO L. CORNELIO BALBO ORATIO. Edited by J. S. REID, Litt. D. 1*s*. 6*d*.

"We are bound to recognize the pains devoted in the annotation of these two orations to the minute and thorough study of their Latinity, both in the ordinary notes and in the textual appendices."—*Saturday Review*.

M. T. CICERONIS PRO P. CORNELIO SULLA ORATIO. Edited by J. S. REID, Litt. D. 3*s*. 6*d*.

"Mr Reid is so well known to scholars as a commentator on Cicero that a new work from him scarcely needs any commendation of ours. His edition of the speech *Pro Sulla* is fully equal in merit to the volumes which he has already published . . . It would be difficult to speak too highly of the notes. There could be no better way of gaining an insight into the characteristics of Cicero's style and the Latinity of his period than by making a careful study of this speech with the aid of Mr Reid's commentary . . . Mr Reid's intimate knowledge of the minutest details of scholarship enables him to detect and explain the slightest points of distinction between the usages of different authors and different periods . . . The notes are followed by a valuable appendix on the text, and another on points of orthography; an excellent index brings the work to a close."—*Saturday Review*.

M. T. CICERONIS PRO CN. PLANCIO ORATIO. Edited by H. A. HOLDEN, LL.D., late Fellow of Trinity College, Cambridge. 4*s*. 6*d*.

"As a book for students this edition can have few rivals. It is enriched by an excellent introduction and a chronological table of the principal events of the life of Cicero; while in its appendix, and in the notes on the text which are added, there is much of the greatest value. The volume is neatly got up, and is in every way commendable."—*The Scotsman*.

M. T. CICERONIS IN Q. CAECILIUM DIVINATIO ET IN C. VERREM ACTIO PRIMA. With Introduction and Notes by W. E. HEITLAND, M.A., and HERBERT COWIE, M.A., Fellows of St John's College, Cambridge. 3*s*.

M. T. CICERONIS ORATIO PRO L. MURENA, with English Introduction and Notes. By W. E. HEITLAND, M.A., Fellow and Classical Lecturer of St John's College, Cambridge. **Second Edition, carefully revised.** 3*s*.

"Those students are to be deemed fortunate who have to read Cicero's lively and brilliant oration for L. Murena with Mr Heitland's handy edition, which may be pronounced 'four-square' in point of equipment, and which has, not without good reason, attained the honours of a second edition."—*Saturday Review.*

M. T. CICERONIS IN GAIUM VERREM ACTIO PRIMA. With Introduction and Notes. By H. COWIE, M.A., Fellow of St John's College, Cambridge. 1*s*. 6*d*.

M. T. CICERONIS ORATIO PRO T. A. MILONE, with a Translation of Asconius' Introduction, Marginal Analysis and English Notes. Edited by the Rev. JOHN SMYTH PURTON, B.D., late President and Tutor of St Catharine's College. 2*s*. 6*d*.

"The editorial work is excellently done."—*The Academy.*

M. T. CICERONIS SOMNIUM SCIPIONIS. With Introduction and Notes. By W. D. PEARMAN, M.A., Head Master of Potsdam School, Jamaica. 2*s*.

P. OVIDII NASONIS FASTORUM LIBER VI. With a Plan of Rome and Notes by A. SIDGWICK, M.A., Tutor of Corpus Christi College, Oxford. 1*s*. 6*d*.

"Mr Sidgwick's editing of the Sixth Book of Ovid's *Fasti* furnishes a careful and serviceable volume for average students. It eschews 'construes' which supersede the use of the dictionary, but gives full explanation of grammatical usages and historical and mythical allusions, besides illustrating peculiarities of style, true and false derivations, and the more remarkable variations of the text."—*Saturday Review.*

"It is eminently good and useful. . . . The Introduction is singularly clear on the astronomy of Ovid, which is properly shown to be ignorant and confused; there is an excellent little map of Rome, giving just the places mentioned in the text and no more; the notes are evidently written by a practical schoolmaster."—*The Academy.*

GAI IULI CAESARIS DE BELLO GALLICO COMMENT. I. II. III. With Maps and English Notes by A. G. PESKETT, M.A., Fellow of Magdalene College, Cambridge. 3*s*.

"In an unusually succinct introduction he gives all the preliminary and collateral information that is likely to be useful to a young student; and, wherever we have examined his notes, we have found them eminently practical and satisfying. . . The book may well be recommended for careful study in school or college."—*Saturday Review.*

"The notes are scholarly, short, and a real help to the most elementary beginners in Latin prose."—*The Examiner.*

—— COMMENT. IV. AND V. AND COMMENT. VII. by the same Editor. 2*s*. each.

—— COMMENT. VI. AND COMMENT. VIII. by the same Editor. 1*s*. 6*d*. each.

London: C. J. CLAY & SON, Cambridge University Press Warehouse, Ave Maria Lane.

P. VERGILI MARONIS AENEIDOS LIBRI I., II., III., IV., V., VI., VII., VIII., IX., X., XI., XII. Edited with Notes by A. SIDGWICK, M.A., Tutor of Corpus Christi College, Oxford. 1*s.* 6*d.* each.

"Much more attention is given to the literary aspect of the poem than is usually paid to it in editions intended for the use of beginners. The introduction points out the distinction between primitive and literary epics, explains the purpose of the poem, and gives an outline of the story." —*Saturday Review.*

"Mr Arthur Sidgwick's 'Vergil, Aeneid, Book XII.' is worthy of his reputation, and is distinguished by the same acuteness and accuracy of knowledge, appreciation of a boy's difficulties and ingenuity and resource in meeting them, which we have on other occasions had reason to praise in these pages."—*The Academy.*

"As masterly in its clearly divided preface and appendices as in the sound and independent character of its annotations. . . . There is a great deal more in the notes than mere compilation and suggestion. . . . No difficulty is left unnoticed or unhandled."—*Saturday Review.*

BOOKS VII. VIII. in one volume. 3*s.*

BOOKS IX. X. in one volume. 3*s.*

BOOKS X., XI., XII. in one volume. 3*s.* 6*d.*

P. VERGILI MARONIS GEORGICON LIBRI I. II. By the same Editor. 2*s.*

QUINTUS CURTIUS. A Portion of the History. (ALEXANDER IN INDIA.) By W. E. HEITLAND, M.A., Fellow and Lecturer of St John's College, Cambridge, and T. E. RAVEN, B.A., Assistant Master in Sherborne School. 3*s.* 6*d.*

"Equally commendable as a genuine addition to the existing stock of school-books is *Alexander in India*, a compilation from the eighth and ninth books of Q. Curtius, edited for the Pitt Press by Messrs Heitland and Raven. . . . The work of Curtius has merits of its own, which, in former generations, made it a favourite with English scholars, and which still make it a popular text-book in Continental schools. . . . . . The reputation of Mr Heitland is a sufficient guarantee for the scholarship of the notes, which are ample without being excessive, and the book is well furnished with all that is needful in the nature of maps, indices, and appendices." —*Academy.*

M. ANNAEI LUCANI PHARSALIAE LIBER PRIMUS, edited with English Introduction and Notes by W. E. HEITLAND, M.A. and C. E. HASKINS, M.A., Fellows and Lecturers of St John's College, Cambridge. 1*s.* 6*d.*

"A careful and scholarlike production."—*Times.*

"In nice parallels of Lucan from Latin poets and from Shakspeare, Mr Haskins and Mr Heitland deserve praise."—*Saturday Review.*

BEDA'S ECCLESIASTICAL HISTORY, BOOKS III., IV., the Text from the very ancient MS. in the Cambridge University Library, collated with six other MSS. Edited, with a life from the German of EBERT, and with Notes, &c. by J. E. B. MAYOR, M.A., Professor of Latin, and J. R. LUMBY, D.D., Norrisian Professor of Divinity. Revised edition. 7*s.* 6*d.*

"To young students of English History the illustrative notes will be of great service, while the study of the texts will be a good introduction to Mediæval Latin."—*The Nonconformist.*

"In Bede's works Englishmen can go back to *origines* of their history, unequalled for form and matter by any modern European nation. Prof. Mayor has done good service in rendering a part of Bede's greatest work accessible to those who can read Latin with ease. He has adorned this edition of the third and fourth books of the 'Ecclesiastical History' with that amazing erudition for which he is unrivalled among Englishmen and rarely equalled by Germans. And however interesting and valuable the text may be, we can certainly apply to his notes the expression, *La sauce vaut mieux que le poisson.* They are literally crammed with interesting information about early English life. For though ecclesiastical in name, Bede's history treats of all parts of the national life, since the Church had points of contact with all."—*Examiner.*

BOOKS I. and II. *In the Press.*

London: C. J. CLAY & SON, Cambridge University Press Warehouse, Ave Maria Lane.

III. FRENCH.

JEANNE D'ARC by A. DE LAMARTINE. With a Map and Notes Historical and Philological and a Vocabulary by Rev. A. C. CLAPIN, M.A., St John's College, Cambridge, and Bachelier-ès-Lettres of the University of France. *2s.*

LE BOURGEOIS GENTILHOMME, Comédie-Ballet en Cinq Actes. Par J.-B. POQUELIN DE MOLIÈRE (1670). With a life of Molière and Grammatical and Philological Notes. By the same Editor. *1s. 6d.*

LA PICCIOLA. By X. B. SAINTINE. The Text, with Introduction, Notes and Map, by the same Editor. *2s.*

LA GUERRE. By MM. ERCKMANN-CHATRIAN. With Map, Introduction and Commentary by the same Editor. *3s.*

LAZARE HOCHE—PAR ÉMILE DE BONNECHOSE. With Three Maps, Introduction and Commentary, by C. COLBECK, M.A., late Fellow of Trinity College, Cambridge. *2s.*

LE VERRE D'EAU. A Comedy, by SCRIBE. With a Biographical Memoir, and Grammatical, Literary and Historical Notes. By the same Editor. *2s.*

"It may be national prejudice, but we consider this edition far superior to any of the series which hitherto have been edited exclusively by foreigners. Mr Colbeck seems better to understand the wants and difficulties of an English boy. The etymological notes especially are admirable. . . . The historical notes and introduction are a piece of thorough honest work."—*Journal of Education.*

HISTOIRE DU SIÈCLE DE LOUIS XIV PAR VOLTAIRE. Part I. Chaps. I.—XIII. Edited with Notes Philological and Historical, Biographical and Geographical Indices, etc. by GUSTAVE MASSON, B.A. Univ. Gallic., Officier d'Académie, Assistant Master of Harrow School, and G. W. PROTHERO, M.A., Fellow and Tutor of King's College, Cambridge. *2s. 6d.*

"Messrs Masson and Prothero have, to judge from the first part of their work, performed with much discretion and care the task of editing Voltaire's *Siècle de Louis XIV* for the 'Pitt Press Series.' Besides the usual kind of notes, the editors have in this case, influenced by Voltaire's 'summary way of treating much of the history,' given a good deal of historical information, in which they have, we think, done well. At the beginning of the book will be found excellent and succinct accounts of the constitution of the French army and Parliament at the period treated of."—*Saturday Review.*

—— Part II. Chaps. XIV.—XXIV. With Three Maps of the Period. By the same Editors. *2s. 6d.*

—— Part III. Chap. XXV. to the end. By the same Editors. *2s. 6d.*

M. DARU, par M. C. A. SAINTE-BEUVE, (Causeries du Lundi, Vol. IX.). With Biographical Sketch of the Author, and Notes Philological and Historical. By GUSTAVE MASSON. *2s.*

LA SUITE DU MENTEUR. A Comedy in Five Acts, by P. CORNEILLE. Edited with Fontenelle's Memoir of the Author, Voltaire's Critical Remarks, and Notes Philological and Historical. By GUSTAVE MASSON. *2s.*

LA JEUNE SIBÉRIENNE. LE LÉPREUX DE LA CITÉ D'AOSTE. Tales by COUNT XAVIER DE MAISTRE. With Biographical Notice, Critical Appreciations, and Notes. By G. MASSON. *2s.*

LE DIRECTOIRE. (Considérations sur la Révolution Française. Troisième et quatrième parties.) Par MADAME LA BARONNE DE STAËL-HOLSTEIN. With a Critical Notice of the Author, a Chronological Table, and Notes Historical and Philological, by G. MASSON, B.A., and G. W. PROTHERO, M.A. Revised and enlarged Edition. 2*s.*

"Prussia under Frederick the Great, and France under the Directory, bring us face to face respectively with periods of history which it is right should be known thoroughly, and which are well treated in the Pitt Press volumes. The latter in particular, an extract from the world-known work of Madame de Staël on the French Revolution, is beyond all praise for the excellence both of its style and of its matter."—*Times.*

DIX ANNÉES D'ÉXIL. LIVRE II. CHAPITRES 1—8. Par MADAME LA BARONNE DE STAËL-HOLSTEIN. With a Biographical Sketch of the Author, a Selection of Poetical Fragments by Madame de Staël's Contemporaries, and Notes Historical and Philological. By GUSTAVE MASSON and G. W. PROTHERO, M.A. Revised and enlarged edition. 2*s.*

FRÉDÉGONDE ET BRUNEHAUT. A Tragedy in Five Acts, by N. LEMERCIER. Edited with Notes, Genealogical and Chronological Tables, a Critical Introduction and a Biographical Notice. By GUSTAVE MASSON. 2*s.*

LE VIEUX CÉLIBATAIRE. A Comedy, by COLLIN D'HARLEVILLE. With a Biographical Memoir, and Grammatical, Literary and Historical Notes. By the same Editor. 2*s.*

"M. Masson is doing good work in introducing learners to some of the less-known French play-writers. The arguments are admirably clear, and the notes are not too abundant."—*Academy.*

LA MÉTROMANIE, A Comedy, by PIRON, with a Biographical Memoir, and Grammatical, Literary and Historical Notes. By the same Editor. 2*s.*

LASCARIS, OU LES GRECS DU XVE. SIÈCLE, Nouvelle Historique, par A. F. VILLEMAIN, with a Biographical Sketch of the Author, a Selection of Poems on Greece, and Notes Historical and Philological. By the same Editor. 2*s.*

LETTRES SUR L'HISTOIRE DE FRANCE (XIII—XXIV.). Par AUGUSTIN THIERRY. By GUSTAVE MASSON, B.A. and G. W. PROTHERO, M.A. With Map. 2*s.* 6*d.*

IV. GERMAN.

DIE KARAVANE von WILHELM HAUFF. Edited with Notes by A. SCHLOTTMANN, Ph. D. 3*s.* 6*d.*

CULTURGESCHICHTLICHE NOVELLEN, von W. H. RIEHL, with Grammatical, Philological, and Historical Notes, and a Complete Index, by H. J. WOLSTENHOLME, B.A. (Lond.). 4*s.* 6*d.*

ERNST, HERZOG VON SCHWABEN. UHLAND. With Introduction and Notes. By H. J. WOLSTENHOLME, B.A. (Lond.), Lecturer in German at Newnham College, Cambridge. 3*s.* 6*d.*

ZOPF UND SCHWERT. Lustspiel in fünf Aufzügen von KARL GUTZKOW. With a Biographical and Historical Introduction, English Notes, and an Index. By the same Editor. 3*s.* 6*d.*

"We are glad to be able to notice a careful edition of K. Gutzkow's amusing comedy 'Zopf and Schwert' by Mr H. J. Wolstenholme. . . . These notes are abundant and contain references to standard grammatical works."—*Academy.*

Goethe's Knabenjahre. (1749—1759.) GOETHE'S BOYHOOD: being the First Three Books of his Autobiography. Arranged and Annotated by WILHELM WAGNER, Ph. D., late Professor at the Johanneum, Hamburg. 2*s.*

HAUFF. DAS WIRTHSHAUS IM SPESSART. Edited by A. SCHLOTTMANN, Ph. D., late Assistant Master at Uppingham School. 3*s*. 6*d*.

DER OBERHOF. A Tale of Westphalian Life, by KARL IMMERMANN. With a Life of Immermann and English Notes, by WILHELM WAGNER, Ph.D., late Professor at the Johanneum, Hamburg. 3*s*.

A BOOK OF GERMAN DACTYLIC POETRY. Arranged and Annotated by the same Editor. 3*s*.

Der erste Kreuzzug (THE FIRST CRUSADE), by FRIEDRICH VON RAUMER. Condensed from the Author's 'History of the Hohenstaufen', with a life of RAUMER, two Plans and English Notes. By the same Editor. 2*s*.

"Certainly no more interesting book could be made the subject of examinations. The story of the First Crusade has an undying interest. The notes are, on the whole, good."—*Educational Times.*

A BOOK OF BALLADS ON GERMAN HISTORY. Arranged and Annotated by the same Editor. 2*s*.

"It carries the reader rapidly through some of the most important incidents connected with the German race and name, from the invasion of Italy by the Visigoths under their King Alaric, down to the Franco-German War and the installation of the present Emperor. The notes supply very well the connecting links between the successive periods, and exhibit in its various phases of growth and progress, or the reverse, the vast unwieldy mass which constitutes modern Germany." —*Times.*

DER STAAT FRIEDRICHS DES GROSSEN. By G. FREYTAG. With Notes. By the same Editor. 2*s*.

"Prussia under Frederick the Great, and France under the Directory, bring us face to face respectively with periods of history which it is right should be known thoroughly, and which are well treated in the Pitt Press volumes."—*Times.*

GOETHE'S HERMANN AND DOROTHEA. With an Introduction and Notes. By the same Editor. Revised edition by J. W. CARTMELL, M.A. 3*s*. 6*d*.

"The notes are among the best that we know, with the reservation that they are often too abundant."—*Academy.*

Das Jahr 1813 (THE YEAR 1813), by F. KOHLRAUSCH. With English Notes. By W. WAGNER. 2*s*.

V. ENGLISH.

SIR THOMAS MORE'S UTOPIA. With Notes by the Rev. J. RAWSON LUMBY, D.D., Norrisian Professor of Divinity; late Fellow of St Catharine's College. 3*s*. 6*d*.

"To Dr Lumby we must give praise unqualified and unstinted. He has done his work admirably. . . . . Every student of history, every politician, every social reformer, every one interested in literary curiosities, every lover of English should buy and carefully read Dr Lumby's edition of the 'Utopia.' We are afraid to say more lest we should be thought extravagant, and our recommendation accordingly lose part of its force."—*The Teacher.*

"It was originally written in Latin and does not find a place on ordinary bookshelves. A very great boon has therefore been conferred on the general English reader by the managers of the *Pitt Press Series*, in the issue of a convenient little volume of *More's Utopia* not in the original Latin, but in the quaint *English Translation thereof made by Raphe Robynson*, which adds a linguistic interest to the intrinsic merit of the work. . . . All this has been edited in a most complete and scholarly fashion by Dr J. R. Lumby, the Norrisian Professor of Divinity, whose name alone is a sufficient warrant for its accuracy. It is a real addition to the modern stock of classical English literature."—*Guardian.*

BACON'S HISTORY OF THE REIGN OF KING HENRY VII. With Notes by the Rev. J. RAWSON LUMBY, D.D. 3*s*.

MORE'S HISTORY OF KING RICHARD III. Edited with Notes, Glossary and Index of Names. By J. RAWSON LUMBY, D.D. Norrisian Professor of Divinity, Cambridge; to which is added the conclusion of the History of King Richard III. as given in the continuation of Hardyng's Chronicle, London, 1543. 3*s*. 6*d*.

THE TWO NOBLE KINSMEN, edited with Introduction and Notes by the Rev. Professor SKEAT, M.A., formerly Fellow of Christ's College, Cambridge. 3*s*. 6*d*.

"This edition of a play that is well worth study, for more reasons than one, by so careful a scholar as Mr Skeat, deserves a hearty welcome."—*Athenæum.*

"Mr Skeat is a conscientious editor, and has left no difficulty unexplained."—*Times.*

LOCKE ON EDUCATION. With Introduction and Notes by the Rev. R. H. QUICK, M.A. 3*s*. 6*d*.

"The work before us leaves nothing to be desired. It is of convenient form and reasonable price, accurately printed, and accompanied by notes which are admirable. There is no teacher too young to find this book interesting; there is no teacher too old to find it profitable."—*The School Bulletin, New York.*

MILTON'S TRACTATE ON EDUCATION. A facsimile reprint from the Edition of 1673. Edited, with Introduction and Notes, by OSCAR BROWNING, M.A., Senior Fellow of King's College, Cambridge, and University Lecturer. 2*s*.

"A separate reprint of Milton's famous letter to Master Samuel Hartlib was a desideratum, and we are grateful to Mr Browning for his elegant and scholarly edition, to which is prefixed the careful *résumé* of the work given in his 'History of Educational Theories.'"—*Journal of Education.*

THEORY AND PRACTICE OF TEACHING. By the Rev. EDWARD THRING, M.A., Head Master of Uppingham School, late Fellow of King's College, Cambridge. New Edition. 4*s*. 6*d*.

"Any attempt to summarize the contents of the volume would fail to give our readers a taste of the pleasure that its perusal has given us."—*Journal of Education.*

GENERAL AIMS OF THE TEACHER, AND FORM MANAGEMENT. Two Lectures delivered in the University of Cambridge in the Lent Term, 1883, by F. W. FARRAR, D.D. Archdeacon of Westminster, and R. B. POOLE, B.D. Head Master of Bedford Modern School. 1*s*. 6*d*.

THREE LECTURES ON THE PRACTICE OF EDUCATION. Delivered in the University of Cambridge in the Easter Term, 1882, under the direction of the Teachers' Training Syndicate. 2*s*.

JOHN AMOS COMENIUS, Bishop of the Moravians. His Life and Educational Works, by S. S. LAURIE, A.M., F.R.S.E., Professor of the Institutes and History of Education in the University of Edinburgh. Second Edition, revised. 3*s*. 6*d*.

OUTLINES OF THE PHILOSOPHY OF ARISTOTLE. Compiled by EDWIN WALLACE, M.A., LL.D. (St Andrews), late Fellow of Worcester College, Oxford. Third Edition Enlarged. 4*s*. 6*d*.

"A judicious selection of characteristic passages, arranged in paragraphs, each of which is preceded by a masterly and perspicuous English analysis."—*Scotsman.*

"Gives in a comparatively small compass a very good sketch of Aristotle's teaching."—*Sat. Review.*

A SKETCH OF ANCIENT PHILOSOPHY FROM THALES TO CICERO, by JOSEPH B. MAYOR, M.A., late Professor of Moral Philosophy at King's College, London. 3*s*. 6*d*.

"Professor Mayor contributes to the Pitt Press Series *A Sketch of Ancient Philosophy* in which he has endeavoured to give a general view of the philosophical systems illustrated by the genius of the masters of metaphysical and ethical science from Thales to Cicero. In the course of his sketch he takes occasion to give concise analyses of Plato's Republic, and of the Ethics and Politics of Aristotle; and these abstracts will be to some readers not the least useful portions of the book."—*The Guardian.*

[*Other Volumes are in preparation.*]

London: C. J. CLAY & SON, Cambridge University Press Warehouse, Ave Maria Lane.